A HISTORY OF BRITAIN IN TEN ENEMIES

www.penguin.co.uk

A HISTORY OF BRITAIN IN TEN ENEMIES

TERRY DEARY

PENGUIN BOOKS

TRANSWORLD PUBLISHERS
Penguin Random House, One Embassy Gardens,
8 Viaduct Gardens, London SW11 7BW
www.penguin.co.uk

Transworld is part of the Penguin Random House group of companies
whose addresses can be found at global.penguinrandomhouse.com

First published in Great Britain in 2024 by Bantam
an imprint of Transworld Publishers
Penguin paperback edition published 2025

Copyright © Terry Deary 2024
Illustrations and map © Diego Abreu

Terry Deary has asserted his right under the Copyright,
Designs and Patents Act 1988 to be identified as the author of this work.

Every effort has been made to obtain the necessary permissions with
reference to copyright material, both illustrative and quoted. We apologize
for any omissions in this respect and will be pleased to make
the appropriate acknowledgements in any future edition.

A CIP catalogue record for this book
is available from the British Library.

ISBN
9781804994979

Text design by Couper Street Type Co.
Typeset in 11.12/15.13pt Adobe Jenson Pro by Jouve (UK), Milton Keynes.
Printed and bound in Great Britain by Clays Ltd, Elcograf S.p.A.

The authorized representative in the EEA is Penguin Random House Ireland,
Morrison Chambers, 32 Nassau Street, Dublin D02 YH68.

Penguin Random House values and supports copyright. Copyright fuels creativity, encourages diverse voices, promotes freedom of expression and supports a vibrant culture. Thank you for purchasing an authorized edition of this book and for respecting intellectual property laws by not reproducing, scanning or distributing any part of it by any means without permission. You are supporting authors and enabling Penguin Random House to continue to publish books for everyone. No part of this book may be used or reproduced in any manner for the purpose of training artificial intelligence technologies or systems. In accordance with Article 4(3) of the DSM Directive 2019/790, Penguin Random House expressly reserves this work from the text and data mining exception.

Penguin Random House is committed to a sustainable future
for our business, our readers and our planet. This book is made
from Forest Stewardship Council® certified paper.

To Jessica, Harry and Oliver Burdess.
The future.

CONTENTS

Introduction   1

1. Italy   13
2. Saxony   51
3. Scandinavia   61
4. France   83
5. Spain   117
6. The Dutch Empire   135
7. United States   153
8. Russia   167
9. Ireland   181
10. Germany   197

Epilogue   225
Further Reading   231
Index   234

THE TEN ENEMIES

1 Italy
2 Saxony
3 Scandinavia
4 France

5 Spain   7 United States   9 Ireland
6 The Dutch Empire   8 Russia   10 Germany

INTRODUCTION

Sheep of a feather flock together. Humans are much the same. They gather into flocks of people who live in the same place and share their language and culture. We call these human flocks 'nations'.

The citizens squabble among themselves, of course. They compete to decide who will be leader of the flock and separate into rival tribes – red, white or blue. They even sometimes threaten to start their own flock with their own rules. Until, that is, a pack of wolves appears to threaten their very existence. Then differences are set aside, a leader emerges, and suddenly the tribes of the nation forget their differences and remember they are all part of the same flock. They unite under their red, white and blue flag and face the enemy.

This is how it is with humans: we are defined not by our friends but by our enemies.

If you win a few battles your self-belief grows. You don't see yourself as any old flock. You see yourself as *the* flock. You see a bit of wolf when you look in the mirror. Maybe you head off to confront other flocks and sample some of their grass.

There's a modest group of islands off the coast of northern Europe. The flock there was divided by the name of their tribe – Iceni or Pict or Silures or Scot. Then along came a wolf-pack that wanted their wealth, and a predictable thing happened: the tribes of the flock set aside their differences and rebelled against the common enemy.

Thousands of years – and at least ten bitter enemies – later, one of those Brits was bold enough to declare: '*The British are special. The world knows it. In our innermost thoughts we know it. This is the greatest nation on Earth.*'

A true nationalist, but not one of Elizabeth I's world conquerors. It was spoken in the last thirty years. By whom? Nigel Farage? No. (I'll tell you later.)

This bloke (there's a clue) is echoing Shakespeare's John of Gaunt, who famously boasted that Britain (and especially England) is a *sceptred isle*, an *earth of majesty*. Not only is it an *other Eden, demi-paradise*, but the rest of the world live in *less happier lands*.

Many Britons today believe that they are different. And when they say 'different' they really mean 'better'. That raises two questions: first, are they right? And second, where did they get that idea from?

A History of Britain in Ten Enemies will try to answer those questions, offering evidence so the reader can make up their own mind as to the place of Britain in today's world. But I hope you'll also find the journey entertaining: the actions of our ancestors were often surprisingly silly.

The Celts who lived in Great Britain called themselves 'Pretani'. Then, when the Romans tried to invade, they invented a goddess of the island, a warrior woman called Britannia. And so for centuries Britain was guarded by a woman armed with a shield and an outsize toasting fork. She was probably meant to be seen as a benevolent goddess who was protective of her people. It could have been a way of encouraging the Britons to accept Roman rule.

To this day, Britannia stands as a symbol of British defiance. We have the Royal Navy's nuclear ballistic missile system, which we named 'Trident'. We also have the song 'Rule, Britannia!', written by James Thomson and set to music by Thomas Arne in 1740. It was originally part of a musical stage show about how Alfred the Great's navy helped defeat the Danes. The British Navy didn't actually command the seas when the song was written. You have to suspect that Thomson borrowed the sentiment from Shakespeare who said, 'This England never did, nor never shall, / Lie at the proud foot of a conqueror'. (It's fair to say the Bard would not have passed GCSE History because England had a track record of being conquered.)

Those words are sung lustily to this day, but they are odd:

When Britain first, at Heaven's command
Arose from out the azure main,
This was the charter of the land,
And guardian angels sang this strain:
'Rule, Britannia! rule the waves:
Britons never will be slaves.'

So God spoke, and Britain rose up out of the blue sea. Why did God do this? She wanted someone to command the seas because She was a bit busy. She was creating night and day, earth and water, the fish of the sea, the fowl of the air, and every living thing that moveth upon the Earth, including a man and a woman in the image of God – a sort of primeval selfie. And all that in the first week. No wonder God said, 'I'm having a bit of trouble with Adam and Eve, a snake and an apple. Can you rule the waves, Britannia, while I Almighty sort out the almighty mess they've made?'

Where did Britannia's prehistoric peoples come from? The most accurate thing we can say is that they all came from somewhere in Europe. These ancient immigrants had no passports or visas, no work permits and paid no tax. We can also be sure they didn't live off tax credits and they weren't medical tourists. Even the British National Party would have let them stay. In 1982 the BNP stated quite clearly, 'Immigration into Britain by non-Europeans should be terminated forthwith, and we should organize a massive programme of repatriation and resettlement overseas of those peoples of non-European origin already resident in this country.' According to their first policy on repatriation that year, 'The British National Party exists to secure a future for the indigenous peoples of these islands in the North Atlantic which have been our homeland for a millennia.'*

So who arrived in Britain first – who are the 'indigenous peoples' who therefore have the right to decide whether or not to allow in 'outsiders'?

The first prehistoric arrivals just wanted to do a bit of hunting and gathering, and faced no newspaper campaign to deport them. They did face hippos, which inhabited the Thames, as well as

---

* A word to the wise. If you plan to promote Britain, then learn to speak its principal *langue* correctly. You can have 'a millennium' (singular) or 'several millennia' (plural) but you can't have 'a millennia'.

mammoths, rhinos and giant beavers. The hunters had invented tools, and soon after that invented endangered species. They could already harness fire — imagine the barbecues you could have with giant beaver. That's why you don't find today's babbling brooks blocked by beaver dams or the motorways slicked by micturating mammoths.

Britain was left unoccupied by humans between one hundred and eighty thousand and sixty thousand years ago. During this period Britain suffered several ice ages, which made it too cold to stick around, with temperatures averaging around -10 degrees Celsius. Sea levels were low enough for an easy crossing back to cosy Europe. Then, as it warmed up, the Neanderthals returned.

These big-brained, beetle-browed boys and girls disappeared forty thousand years ago, not long after *Homo sapiens* arrived in Europe. Neanderthals couldn't compete for Britain's resources and today they are generally believed to be extinct, though there are reports of sightings in a place called the House of Lords.

Modern humans strolled to and fro across a land bridge connecting what's now the Netherlands to East Anglia, before it flooded around 6000 BC. The hunters used natural features like cliffs to drive wild animals to their deaths and eat them. The idea was certainly around in France in 18000 BC, when there is evidence that horses were driven over cliffs and finished off with a bludgeon to the brain (perhaps they used a pony club). Then, around 4000 BC, farmers arrived from Europe to plant crops and domesticate animals.

The ancient Brits were spiritual. They looked after their dead. In west Britain, tombs were built out of stone and hidden under mounds of rubble; in the stoneless east the dead were buried under long barrows (mounds of earth over timber houses). Fussell's Lodge in Wiltshire, on the edge of Salisbury Plain, was created around 3630 BC. It's a long barrow with a timber house that held the remains of over fifty people (and an ox skull). The building was covered in a mound of chalk. Most of the bodies were buried shortly after death, but some died quite a while before their remains were interred. At one end of the long barrow there was usually a 'mortuary house'. That's where a dead body would be left to rot till the flesh fell off and the bones were scraped clean before they were buried. Nice work for the undertaker.

These hefty-but-holy men and women littered the landscape with wooden henges. No planning permission was sought. They got around using dug-out boats carved from tree trunks (canoe believe it?), spreading across Britain. But the population was in decline until in 2500 BC the Beaker people arrived.

These beaker-making farmers traced their origins to Turkey. Soon they would replace most of the old British natives. Wood henges were modernized into stone henges. They buried their dead with stylized bell-shaped pots, copper daggers, arrowheads and stone wrist guards and made unusual perforated buttons. The Stone Age Britons were swamped by the immigrants.

Stonehenge is still there today and – a bit like the mystery of Jack the Ripper – there are new theories every year. Some are brilliant, many are batty. Who Built Stonehenge? Pick your theory:

- Stonehenge is about the same age as the pyramids so it must have been built by Egyptians.

- Stonehenge was built by priests from a Mediterranean island in 1600 BC.
- Stonehenge is the site of the Garden of Eden.
- Stonehenge was built by aliens as a launch pad for their spaceships. Using only stones.

The theories as to why it was built are too numerous to list in full. A giant calendar? A gateway to the land of the dead? We don't know for certain. We do, however, know the odd story of how it came into public ownership.

In 1915 Cecil Chubb, a rich barrister, went to an auction in a Salisbury theatre to buy a pair of curtains. At the auction, Stonehenge was put up for sale by the aristocratic Antrobus family who'd owned it for generations. Cecil began bidding for Stonehenge. Why? Some say it was a birthday present for his wife. Maybe she liked necklaces and rings, and asked for something unique featuring big stones? Others say he was stirred by his love of Britannia and bid to stop a foreign chap getting his hands on a piece of British history.

Three years later Chubb gifted the site to the nation. The Brit people got Stonehenge; Cecil got a knighthood. (There is no record of him getting his curtains.)

By 1200 BC, more than a thousand years after Stonehenge was erected, people began to live in villages. The Britons congregated in tribes and many built hill forts. You'd only erect defences if you were afraid of being attacked, so these tribes must have had rivalries, maybe about land but probably about wealth. Trade with those foreigners on the continent was growing, and the Brit tribal chiefs became the fat cats of Bronze Age Britain. Their tombs were opulent. The chiefs were dead rich – but still dead.

By 750 BC the Iron Age was beginning and there were about one hundred and fifty thousand inhabitants in Britain. You'd require two Wembley Stadiums to fit them in. Britain needed more immigrants to grow. But around 500 BC bands of rather aggressive immigrants arrived, known as the Celts. Some historians believe the Celts worshipped certain trees, believing that the natural world contained spirits. You could pray to rocks, streams and mountains – but trying to get a reply from a mountain is an uphill struggle.

There was no uniting of the tribes to repel these incomers. There was no 'Britannia' yet. The underpopulated islands simply absorbed the Celts. Or maybe the Celts *were* the Beaker People. Historians are still squabbling. Let's not get involved.

What we can say is that a more warlike bunch of immigrants drifted into Britannia's green and pleasant land. By 300 BC swords were making their appearance in place of daggers. Where there's wealth there's someone out there who wants to relieve the rich of it. And Britain was rich in tin, particularly in Cornwall. Once you'd used your new sword to kill someone for a few newfangled coins, you wouldn't bury them. Some corpses were now chargrilled – or, as more PC people prefer to call it, cremated.

As well as cremation, Celts brought some nasty habits with them. Nasty habits like sacrifices.

Legend says that the city of Bath, long before the Romans arrived to build their famous baths, was founded by the British prince Bladud. The poor lad contracted leprosy so he was exiled to be a swineherd (a boaring job). When the swine caught leprosy they ran into the mud and were cured – Bladud copied the swine and he was cured. He returned to be king of the Brits. And miraculous Bath became a place to make sacrifices.

Many of the 'facts' about Celts come from later Roman chroniclers who wanted to make the Romans look 'civilized' in comparison. The Romans claimed the Celts believed that severed heads could speak, tell the future and give you warnings. Celts (they said) claimed that dead heads were extra-powerful in groups of three, and they had several goddesses with three heads including Morrígan, an Irish goddess of war and fate. Each head represented a different aspect of her nature – battle, death and prophecy. With that kind of workload, three heads are better than one.

The Celts really believed in the power of the head. They stuck rotting heads on poles at the gates of their hill forts. They threw heads into lakes and rivers as a gift to the gods and nailed enemy heads to their walls as a sort of decoration. Celts kept enemy heads pickled so they could be taken out and looked at by visitors as a grim conversation piece.

Modern archaeology confirms that Celts buried some of their dead with the head removed and placed between the legs. There is no definitive answer as to why they did this. Some say the Celts believed that the head was the seat of the soul, and that by removing it and placing it there they were ensuring that the soul would be reborn. So maybe it was a show of affection: 'You're dead, mate, come back soon. Missing you already.'

An alternative – and contradictory – suggestion is that the Celts believed that the head was a source of power, and that by removing it and placing it between the legs they were preventing the deceased from using that power to harm the living. More a way of saying, 'You are dead. Please stay dead and don't haunt your old pals.'

The sensible explanation is that the Celts simply buried their dead in this way because it was the most efficient method of saving space. Land was becoming more scarce, so burying the dead in a crouched position with their head removed would have allowed for more bodies to be buried in a restricted space. They missed a trick if they didn't realize that burying corpses vertically would save most space of all ('Standing room only').

The Romans claimed the Celts had sacred groves where they worshipped at temples in the trees. There is no archaeology to back this up, since the trees have rotted and the Romans flattened the temples they found on arrival. The invaders even had the cheek to build Roman temples on the sites of the British ones.

As part of the propaganda war, the Romans wrote that the Celtic Brits enjoyed a bit of human sacrifice. Julius Caesar said that slaves would be burnt along with the body of their master as part of his funeral rites in order to improve their crops. He also claimed that they built wicker figures that were filled with living humans and then burnt. A good subject for a horror film.* Although different Celtic gods preferred different styles of sacrifice. Esus liked his victims hanged, while Teutates preferred them drowned, like the Lindow Man.

---

* In *The Wicker Man*, Police Sergeant Howie delivers the timeless line, 'Don't you see that killing me is not going to bring back your apples?' He was right. Granny Smith was dead, and soon Sergeant Howie would be too. Just another baked being.

INTRODUCTION

In 1984 a mechanical digger was cutting through turf in Lindow, Cheshire, when it came across a shrivelled body. Archaeologists and historians were excited (they are sick people, you understand). They examined the body and said it was definitely a Celt. The chemicals in the swampy land had preserved him like a pickled onion. The one and only ancient Celtic face to be seen in modern times. Who was he and how did he end up in a bog?

The man had well-shaped fingernails, so he wasn't a peasant. His death seems to have been some sort of cut-throat Celtic sacrifice to get help from their gods to fight the Romans. Or the Lindow Man could have agreed to be sacrificed to help his people. We'll never be sure, but he'd been bashed on the head, strangled, had his throat cut and was thrown into the bog to drown (if he wasn't already dead by then).

What would you do if you found the corpse of Lindow Man, who was killed and dumped in a bog? Would you give him a nice burial and let him rest in peace? Of course you would. What did the historians do with him? They stuck him in a glass case at the British Museum for people to gawp at.

The Celts didn't all die in a battle or a bog. Infant mortality was high, as you may expect in the days before the NHS rode to our rescue. Fairies were always on the lookout for newborn babies to steal. When a baby died young, the wise ones in the tribe said the *real* child had been stolen and it was the changeling that had died. To protect her child, a mother had to make a fire (maybe by burning peat) and carry it clockwise round the child, morning and night. Fire frightens fairies.

If you want to be a lucky Celt, try to make sure you are born on a Monday. Friday is an unlucky day, so don't get yourself born on a Friday. ('Unlucky Friday' then became a tradition in many Christian countries as the day of the Crucifixion.) The unlucky ones that died weren't always cremated, depending on the fashion of the time. Some were placed on a board and had soil and salt sprinkled on their chests. If a cat or dog walked over the corpse, then the creature had to be killed instantly. The body was taken to the graveyard in a wicker coffin with a hinged bottom. It was lowered into the grave, the base was opened up and the dear departed dumped. The coffin could then be reused. So it seems the Celts were the first people to introduce recycling into the funeral trade.

Whatever else we can say about these enigmatic Celts, they were not the first to arrive, and they wouldn't be the last. It may have been their tribalism which led to their downfall. The English clergyman Sabine Baring-Gould (1834–1924) wrote that 'the tribal system, from which the Celt never freed himself entirely, was the curse of the Celtic race, predooming it to ruin'. And ruin was on the way. It took the form of a rampaging empire known to history as the Romans.

The first of Britain's great enemies was named after a child who was rescued and suckled by a wolf. When the wolves descended on the Britannic sheep, it almost made them flock together in defiance. Almost.

1
ITALY

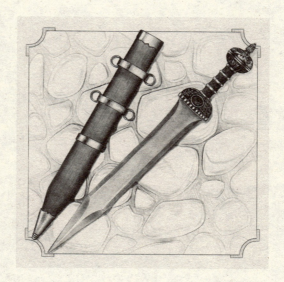

The Celtic tribes of Britain were not in any position to unite against a common enemy when the Romans arrived. They were, at least, great warriors, fighting in formidable tribal war-bands. They fought naked and painted blue. (Or they might have simply turned blue in the British climate.) But the Romans said the Celts wore a blue dye called woad. For all their fearsomeness, Celt warriors fought as individuals while the Romans fought in units, making the Celts vulnerable in the face of Roman military discipline.

The Romans painted the Celts as savages. But the Romans were not exactly well mannered. The Roman historian Tacitus (AD 56–120) had a low opinion of his contemporaries, saying that 'Rome was a magnet for the atrocious and shameless.' I'd argue that the Roman Empire was the most vicious and murderous of ancient times. What other empire killed humans for sport and invited fifty thousand citizens to watch, cheer and enjoy?

Britannia has a long memory. Her history remembers offences that other nations committed centuries or even millennia ago. And the sense of distrust lingers in the national psyche. Enmities against Italy go back to the Roman invasions. And other nations remember their grievances against Britannia just as vividly – will

Greece ever forget that the Brits nicked her marbles? By now we're happy to integrate them – having been brought round by ice-cream parlours, espresso, Ferraris, spaghetti Bolognese and the Mediterranean diet that lets you live to a hundred without really trying. But the peoples from the place we now call Italy haven't always been so welcome on Britannia's shores.

First to arrive was Julius Caesar. He wisely wrote his own memoirs, an unreliable kind of book created to make the author look good. At least he believed the islands of Britannia existed. For Britannia lay at the edge of the Romans' known world, a land of great mystery. Pytheas of Massalia (*fl.* 320–306 BC) had been the first person to describe Britannia and his travels there, but some Roman writers insisted that the place did not exist and dismissed the chronicles of Pytheas as a hoax. That was all about to change.

The first to confront the Roman invaders were the Cassivellauni tribe who lived in the area we now call London. The first notable British king had been Lud, the legends say. He built a town north of the Thames, and it was named after him: Luddum, which in time Brits' twisted tongues turned into London. They say Lud is buried near the place we now call Ludgate. A crumbling effigy of King Lud once stood on the gate. Now that statue stands in the porch of the Church of St Dunstan-in-the-West on Fleet Street instead.

Lud's son, Cassivellaunus, became the Celtic king of the region. His people squabbled with the other tribes along the Thames, until the Romans appeared across the river. Cassivellaunus united many of the local tribes to fight them, falling back on the old concept that 'my enemy's enemy is my friend'. That 'enemy's enemy' idea was even older than Lud. It appears in the *Arthashastra*, an ancient Indian discourse on statecraft and military strategy written by the teacher Kautilya in the 400s BC.* The idea has been used by many leaders throughout history, from Machiavelli to Churchill. It can be used to justify alliances of convenience, teaming up with distasteful partners who would normally be antagonistic. Common sense says that 'my enemy's enemy is my friend' is not always true. The enemy of my enemy is just another enemy. We'll never know what the British tribal allies of the Cassivellauni thought of this alliance of convenience because we see the conflict through the eyes of Julius Caesar. At last, there was a semblance of a force that could be called 'British', defined by his account.

Caesar's neat catchphrase '*Veni, vidi, vici*' – I came, I saw, I conquered – was first used in a message to the Roman Senate, written in 46 BC in the city of Zela, in the area now known as Tokat Province, Turkey. He didn't get to use his catchphrase nine years earlier when he took on cool Britannia ... and lost. He would not be the last Mediterranean visitor to be beaten by the British weather.

It was in 55 BC (late August) that Julius made his first expedition to Britain. He'd defeated troublesome tribes in Gaul but believed their leaders had fled to Britain to hide. As Caesar didn't say (not even in Latin), 'You can run but you can't hide.'† Caesar

---

* Some scholars say the *Arthashastra* was actually the creation of several authors over centuries.
† That was a line from heavyweight boxing champion Joe Louis, just before his 1946 victory over the lighter, faster Billy Conn.

tried to pump merchants across the Channel for intelligence – the disposition of British tribes, good invasion sites and so on. The merchants (who had a good thing going as they traded between Gaul and Britain) weren't very helpful; indeed, they warned the Brits that Caesar planned to invade, giving the tribes time to organize a defence along the south-east coast.

Caesar sailed with a large force but was greeted by massed forces of Britons gathered on the white cliffs. Javelins could be thrown down on to anyone landing there. Far less pleasant than bluebirds over the white cliffs of Dover. Caesar sailed along the south coast, tracked by British defenders. He hadn't thought this through. The ships were so loaded with men, weapons and supplies that they sat low in the water and couldn't be run up on to the beaches. The invaders would have to jump into deep water while being pelted by Brits.

Eventually they landed at Pegwell Bay on the eastern tip of Kent. Legend has it that a standard-bearer of the X Legion jumped in first as an example, shouting: 'Leap, fellow soldiers, unless you wish to betray your eagle to the enemy. I, for my part, will perform my duty to the republic and to my general.' They leapt. Their horses didn't. Storms and tides made a cavalry landing impossible, so the Romans couldn't ride on to London – they'd have to hike.

There were bloody skirmishes in the days that followed. Caesar demanded hostages. Only two tribes sent them because they didn't feel particularly threatened by these all-conquering Romans. Caesar's forces also had problems foraging for food in the unfamiliar British countryside. There wasn't a spaghetti tree in sight.

After about a week in Britain, Caesar decided to withdraw. A week? What sort of superpower throws in the towel – even a very wet one – after a week? This was the first recorded time – but not the last – that Britain was saved by a combination of the legendary white cliffs of Dover and the even more legendary British weather. Caesar claimed he had achieved his main goal of gathering intelligence about the Britons and his show of force would deter tribal warlords like Cassivellaunus from raiding Gaul. But the truth is he could not have been a happy Caesar. He came, he saw, he went home with wet feet.

In 54 BC (July) Julius made a second expedition to Britain. He was more ambitious this time, and he'd brought a much greater force. Empires are like untied party balloons; you have to keep on expanding. If you stop blowing you shrink pretty quickly. Caesar knew that. He probably also sensed that, like a party balloon, when you get too big your balloon empire will burst spectacularly and suddenly. All empires have in the past. It seems to be a law of nature. But Caesar reckoned the Roman Empire was nowhere near its apogee – its bursting point. Caesar wanted to expand Roman influence into Britain. He was an ambitious man, and he saw the invasion as an opportunity to increase his own prestige and power.

He was backed by the powerful leaders back home in Rome because a victory would gain Roman access to Britain's natural resources: rich deposits of tin and copper. Then there were the human resources. Caesar believed that Britain had a large population, which could provide a source of slaves and recruits for the Roman Army. Empires are run for the benefit of the rulers, and profits are greater if you don't have to pay the menials who keep the empire running. Force your defeated enemies into slavery and you get a cheap source of servants and farm labourers, the men who drive the carts to market and the women who empty your latrines.

Some of the British tribes wanted to hitch their wagon to the Roman star and weren't as committed to the defence of their islands. They didn't appreciate what a Roman occupation would mean for them. Caesar was happy to adopt the old tactic 'divide and conquer', a concept that was at least three hundred years old by the time Caesar arrived on the shores of Britain for a second time. The phrase is attributed to Philip II of Macedon, who used it to describe his method of rule from 359 to 336 BC. Mind you, Philip was so busy dividing and conquering his enemies he wasn't watching his friends and family. He was assassinated at the age of forty-six – maybe with the connivance of his son, Alexander the Great.

Caesar may not have coined the phrase *'divide et impera'*, but he was the master of employing its wisdom. He'd learnt from his failure the year before. He had more men (five legions instead of two), more cavalry and landing craft suited to the job. He also had some secret weapons.

He came, he saw, he landed and set off for London. But the good old British weather battered his fleet of landing ships after they had disgorged the legionaries. Forty vessels were lost and a quick retreat was no longer an option (unless his soldiers could swim the Channel). Caesar halted and for ten days repaired his fleet.

Then he was off north again. He described the British resistance tactics in his memoirs. In essence the British fighters took a taxi ride on a chariot to the battlefront. Caesar said, 'In chariot fighting the Britons begin by driving all over the field hurling javelins, and generally the terror inspired by the horses and the noise of the wheels is sufficient to throw their opponents' ranks into disorder. Then, after making their way between the squadrons of their own cavalry, they jump down from the chariot and engage on foot.' The charioteers hung around in case their passengers wanted a quick lift back to safety. Caesar was impressed by the Brit driving abilities: 'They can run along the chariot pole, stand on the yoke, and get back into the chariot as quick as lightning.' Smart circus skills.

The invaders pressed on through Kent to London, lining up on the south bank of the Thames. Cassivellaunus, leader of the combined tribal forces, and his Britons stood with swords and spears on the north bank. Caesar probably aimed to cross the river at Westminster. The stories he'd heard from the Gaul armies had persuaded Cassivellaunus that he couldn't win a pitched battle, so he would wage guerrilla warfare. But the Romans had something bigger than a gorilla.

The British waited, daring the Romans to cross. Their fierce faces were painted blue. Caesar spoke to his legions: 'Even now, we can still turn back. But once we have crossed that river, we will have to fight.' A challenge to the courage of his men. Who could resist it? (In fact, it went down so well that he reused the idea when he crossed the Rubicon five years later.) Then, from the south came a monster that even Father Thames hadn't seen for thousands of years. Caesar's secret weapon. A war elephant, in plate armour and with a tower on its back from which arrows and slingshot could be fired.

Cassivellaunus beat a sneaky retreat in the face of the powerful pachyderm. He was isolated. He had upset too many of his neighbours by expanding his own power and territory through conquest. On that old principle of 'my enemy's enemy is my friend', those offended neighbours offered help to Caesar. And, of course, fear of Rome persuaded many tribes to ingratiate themselves with Caesar. They revealed where Cassivellaunus was hiding, and Caesar forced the Brit boss to negotiate a peace. Britannia was a geographic location, but it was not yet a nation. It was the tribal rivalries of the Celts, as much as Caesar's war-machine, that defeated Cassivellaunus.

Yet Caesar was nervous. At any moment storms could cut him off from his European base, causing huge logistical problems for supplying his men. The increased number of legions had helped him get a foothold but also meant more mouths to feed. And keeping a pet elephant fed was a jumbo task for any commander (they can eat about 150kg of food a day). Caesar and his legions went home to Rome before the winter left him stranded in Britain.

'I came, I saw, I made a few friends. They will be a useful fifth column when Claudius invades around ninety years after I've been stabbed in the back.'

Tacitus put Caesar's invasions into context when he wrote, 'It was, in fact, the deified Julius who first of all Romans entered

Britain with an army: he overawed the natives by a successful battle and made himself master of the coast; but it may be said that he revealed, rather than bequeathed, Britain to Rome.'

Rome had a direct line to Britain and her warlords now. They had an even better idea of what it would take to conquer the divided people. They knew who their Britannic friends were too. They'd be back. It might surprise us that it took almost a century, but they had their hands full elsewhere. In the intervening years the Roman legions had their noses bloodied at battles like the Teutoburg Forest in AD 9, when a coalition of 'friendly' Germanic tribes led by Arminius annihilated three Roman legions and their auxiliaries in the Teutoburg Forest.

Arminius was a Germanic officer who had served in the Roman Army. He took Roman citizenship and received a Roman military education. He may have had ambitions to be the paramount leader of Gaul and a rebellion against the occupiers would be a major step on the stairway to the top. His Roman education gave him the knowledge and skills to deceive the Roman commander, Publius Quinctilius Varus, and anticipate the Roman Army's tactics. Varus and his legions were lured into a maze of forest paths where they couldn't deploy in their usual battle formations. That would be because they didn't expect a battle – the forest route was just a shortcut to get to where they thought there was a rebellion to be crushed. The Romans were ambushed and destroyed. The guts of the Roman soldiers were strung from the trees and Varus fell on his sword – literally – while his uncle the Roman emperor Augustus was left sobbing and banging his head against the marble walls of his palace as he cried out,

'Publius Quinctilius Varus, bring me back my legions.' The walls were undamaged, and Varus didn't have any legions to bring back, so it was a pretty pointless gesture.

The Battle of the Teutoburg Forest had a significant impact on German history as it helped to forge a sense of shared identity among the Germanic tribes, who would come for Britain eventually. It also had a profound impact on the Roman Empire. It forced the Romans to abandon their plans to conquer Germania and it marked the end of Roman expansion into northern Europe – unless it turned to those damp little islands they called Britannia, of course.

But the British tribes did not heed the lessons: that Roman armies could be defeated and that unity – that national identity – could stand against a ruthless empire. And they didn't have an Arminius.

If the tribes of Britain had had history teachers they could have pointed out to the warlords and warladies that the way to defeat the Romans was to imitate Arminius, fighting them on your own terms and your own battlegrounds using guerrilla tactics. Never, never face them in a pitched battle. But there were no British history teachers yet.

Our first-century teacher may also have sounded another warning to the British chieftains: if you do defeat the Roman invader, then remember that an alliance of the tribes was a temporary agreement to confront a common enemy. Don't, dear chieftain, get carried away and think you are automatically going to assume leadership of a united nation. That is what Arminius did. The hero of Teutoburg Forest became too big for his boots and his fellow tribal leaders resented it. Arminius died in AD 21, twelve years after defeating the Romans, assassinated by his fellow Germanic tribesmen. He'd become so ruthless his compatriots saw him as no better than Varus. And so, they decided, Arminius deserved the same fate.

In AD 43 the Romans, under Emperor Claudius, returned to Britannia. This time they stayed for a few hundred years. Like many invaders throughout history, they claimed they had to do it – they were not the aggressors. The Atrebates tribe were friendly to Rome and were attacked by Caratacus, king of the Catuvellauni. The king of the Atrebates went crying to the new Roman emperor, Claudius, and asked him to help them. Claudius was spoiling for a fight. A foreign victory always made an emperor look strong and popular. Claudius had his excuse to invade Britannia.

The greatest warrior of a Celtic tribe liked to fight alone, as a champion – not as part of an army. He dressed in his finest jewels of gold and glass and no clothes but his breeches, standing at the front of the battlefield, beating his sword against his shield.

When an enemy champion stepped forward to answer his challenge, they fought. Often to the death. And the winner took the courage of his dead enemy by cutting off his head. When the rest of the tribe joined in they were no better than a rabble, a mob, just a gang of farmers and peasants led by chiefs on chariots. They fought to the death because a Celt would not run away. They believed they died and were born again as another person. (That's what their Druid priests told them.) So the bodies covered the battlefields like leaves in autumn.

The Romans had no truck with this custom. Roman soldiers

stayed in their tight groups and marched like a tide that couldn't be stopped. They washed away the scattered tribes. When Claudius' legions landed they drove Caratacus and his Catuvellauni back to their base in Colchester. From there, Caratacus went visiting as many tribes as he could to find warriors who would fight with him.

Meanwhile, the legions paused at Colchester so a VIP could witness their capturing the Catuvellauni city. That important person was no less than Emperor Claudius himself. The Romans with their catapults quickly took Colchester and the tribes of southern Britain soon submitted while Caratacus made a sharp exit. Better fled than dead. He got to the area we now call Cardiff in the summer of AD 48 and stirred up the people down in the South West to fight a guerrilla war.

When Caratacus arrived, he encountered the people of Caerau hill fort, the Silures. Together they attacked the tribes, like the Dubonni, that had surrendered to the Romans. They put them to the fire and the sword. Naturally the Romans arrived in Wales, looking to capture Caratacus. The Roman general Publius Scapula (AD 15–52) wanted to fight a regular pitched battle because that's what the Romans were good at. The Silures wanted to raid Roman camps and attack Roman supply wagons on the wild Welsh roads. Guerrilla warfare just as Arminius would have advocated.

Despite fighting tactically, by AD 50 the Silures' army was weakened by the constant low-level conflict. Caratacus and his fighters moved north to get help from the Ordovices tribe. That left the ordinary Silures people in Cardiff with nobody to fight for them. The ruthless Roman general Scapula had an idea: he wanted every single Silures tribe member moved to Roman camps or killed.

He ordered the Roman troops to follow Caratacus into the mountains of Wales. The rebel Brit decided this was a good place to make his last stand against the legions. Caratacus fought a great final battle – of course, he lost. As Tacitus said: 'It was a glorious Roman victory. The wife and daughter of Caratacus were captured, and his brothers surrendered.' Caratacus did the same thing he usually did: he ran away to find another tribe that would join his fight against Rome. He reached the Brigantes, living up in the area we now call Yorkshire and ruled by Queen Cartimandua. But sadly, Cartimandua was *friends* with the invaders. She 'helped' Caratacus into shackles and chains and handed him over to the Romans.

Scapula – the enemy of the Silures – died soon after he captured Caratacus, 'worn out with care'. The Silures, deserted by Caratacus, carried on fighting, brave but pretty much alone. It would take another twenty-five years and two more Roman generals before the Silures were finally crushed.

As for Caratacus, he was taken to Rome to be strangled. But Caratacus by now had quite a lot of practice evading death. He said to Emperor Claudius, 'I am the first great hero of the Britons. I'm no good *dead* and *buried*. Let me live and it will show the world how great you are. I will be a *living* sign of your greatness.'

He lived.

Over the next twenty years the Romans spread northward and westward, achieving pretty much what Julius Caesar had hoped for when he laid the ground with his invasions.

The tribes of Wales continued to harass the Romans, aided by the local fighting gods. The Celt priests, the Druids, offered their gods gifts by throwing precious objects or weapons into a river or a bog. Maybe the gods lived there, or maybe they were expected to get wet and muddy fishing the gifts out. The gifts included jewellery and a lot of weapons.*

In AD 60 the Roman general and governor Paulinus had to march north to deal with them. His legionaries faced a scary sight at Anglesey. Tacitus described it: 'On the far shore stood the forces of the enemy, a dense show of arms and men, with women dashing through the ranks like the furies; their dress was black, their hair dishevelled, and they carried torches in their hands. The Druids stood round the fighting men, pouring forth horrible curses, with their hands uplifted towards the heavens. They struck terror into the Roman soldiers by the strangeness of the sight; it was as if the Roman limbs were frozen, they could not move.'

Paulinus and his Romans already controlled the land from the Wash to the Severn Estuary with his veterans. It was the tribes of Anglesey that needed to be taught a lesson. But the combination of Druids and women scared the legionaries.

Tacitus was a bit of a sycophant, so of course he made Paulinus sound like a hero: 'The brave Paulinus said they would not be scared by a rabble of women and madmen.' The Roman infantry were inspired by his speech and crossed the Menai Straits into Anglesey on specially designed flat-bottomed boats while the

---

* You can imagine a Celt warrior being told to bring his sword to fight the invaders. 'Sorry, I left it in the bog.'

cavalry swam across on their horses. The Welsh thought they'd be safe from the Romans behind the watery barrier, but the Romans overcame the problem and attacked. Tacitus went on: 'They smote all the Welsh and wrapped them in the flames the Welsh had lit. The Romans killed everyone who stood in their way, including the women and Druids who carried no weapons.'

The Romans tore down the sacred temples where the Druids had carried out their sacrifices. Tacitus said the Romans found the trees dripping with human blood. They then turned the tables on the enemy by drenching their sacrificial altars in Druid blood. The entrails of the victims fell to the woodland floor.

Then Paulinus received word of an Iceni rebellion over in East Anglia. He hadn't seen it coming. Maybe he ought to have consulted the entrails.

Britannia was subdued, but it still wasn't a British state – the tribes were simply 'clients' of Rome. And so it could have remained if the Romans hadn't mistreated the wrong woman.

The story may be familiar. Boudicca was queen of the Iceni people of eastern England. She was married to King Prasutagus, and when the Romans invaded England in AD 43 they allowed Prasutagus to keep his throne. Inconsiderately, Prasutagus died, and the Romans decided to rule the Iceni directly. They were accused of stripping and flogging Boudicca then raping her daughters. As Prime Minister Margaret Thatcher would later argue, 'What Britain needs is an iron lady.'* When Paulinus set

---

* The phrase 'Iron Lady' originated in a 1976 article in the Soviet Army newspaper *Red Star*. The article was critical of Thatcher's foreign

off to battle the people of Anglesey, Boudicca took the opportunity to lead a rebellion.

According to the eloquent Roman scribes, Boudicca was a tall, fierce-looking woman with long red hair and a harsh voice. She is said to have worn a brightly coloured tunic and a thick cloak fastened with a brooch, and to have carried a spear when she spoke to her people. Tacitus describes Boudicca as a woman of 'great spirit and intelligence' who was 'not to be lightly despised'. He also writes that she was a 'skilled orator' who was able to rally her people to fight against the Romans. Cassius Dio (164–c.235) said Boudicca was a 'woman of extraordinary beauty and stature, with piercing blue eyes and a tawny mane of hair'. He also said she was 'a natural leader' who was able to inspire her people to fight for their freedom. But we need to be wary of an enemy's description of an opponent: the greater your enemy, the greater your victory.

We can be sure that Boudicca was a warrior queen of the Iceni tribe which occupied the modern English counties of Norfolk and Suffolk, as well as parts of Cambridgeshire, Hertfordshire and Essex. Boudicca persuaded her neighbours to set aside their differences and join her in driving out the common enemy.

They donned their warpaint of woad™ and set out to murder as many Romans as they could. They picked a soft target to start with, Colchester. The city was new and its walls were made of

---

policy, and it described her as a 'steely-nerved, unflinching leader' who was 'determined to crush the working class'. The phrase was quickly picked up by the British press, and Thatcher chose to embrace the nickname, portraying herself as a strong and decisive leader.

earth and wood. It had a small Roman garrison but not one large enough to defend the city against a major attack. It was located in a relatively isolated area, far from the nearest Roman legion in Gloucester, several days' march away.

Before we hail Boudicca as a feminist icon, we should look at the account of Cassius Dio. He writes that Boudicca's rebels were especially cruel to women prisoners. Roman residents' wives and daughters were hung up naked, had their breasts cut off and sewed to their mouths. The cadavers were then impaled, having a sharp wooden stake pushed through their bodies, and they were raised up for the triumphant Brit tribes to exult. Tacitus said, 'The Britons couldn't wait to cut throats, hang, and burn and crucify.'

The IX Legion marched to the relief of Colchester. These hardened pros intended to sort out the natives. But they were ambushed and butchered. They were too late to save the Colchester Romans anyway. The leaders fled on their horses; the poor foot soldiers were left to their fate.

Boudicca's troops left Colchester a smoking ruin and headed for London – the Smoke. An apt nickname. Paulinus evacuated the city before Boudicca lit up the town. Tacitus writes, 'Near the mouth of the Thames there appeared a ruined town; even the sea had taken on the colour of blood. When the tide went out, you could see shapes like human forms in the mud.' The Londoners were left to the mercy of Boudicca's rebels just as the IX Legion foot soldiers had been and with the same result. Archaeologists have unearthed decapitated cockneys, men and women, from this era. In 1988 a site near the Houses of Parliament in Westminster was excavated and uncovered the remains of a Roman-era cemetery. The bodies had been hastily buried. 'Mercy' wasn't in the Iceni dictionary (if they'd had one).

Boudicca then turned back north, burning her bridges (literally). Paulinus let the rebels have St Albans. As he marched from one Roman settlement to another he was gathering troops all the time, amassing around ten thousand. Boudicca was gathering more: around two hundred and thirty thousand, one source claimed. Do the maths.

As Iron Lady Thatcher said of a conflict in the Falkland Islands, 'Defeat? I do not recognize the meaning of the word.' It could have been a quote from Boudicca. But defeat was a word Boudicca would have to add to the Iceni dictionary, because she met it at the Battle of Watling Street in the south Midlands.

Her rebellion had been a major success in pulling the disparate tribes of Britain together. She had maybe one hundred thousand warriors under her command (a more credible number). The British were fuelled by hatred. The Romans relied on tactics. Unlike Arminius at the Teutoburg Forest, Boudicca did not choose the battleground and she let the Romans fight in battle formation. All she had in her favour was a numerical advantage – but a considerable one if Roman sources are to be believed.

Paulinus must have remembered the old tale of Horatius Cocles, an officer in the army of the ancient Roman Republic, who had famously defended the Pons Sublicius from an invading army. Cocles had funnelled the enemy though a narrow attacking front to minimize their numerical advantage. Paulinus chose to defend a narrow gorge, waiting for the attacking Brits to come to them, impaling themselves on Roman spears and swords. To make matters worse, the British tribes had brought along women and children to watch the sport and they formed a line of supply carts behind their fighters. Unfortunately (or stupidly), that line of carts blocked the retreat of the Brits when the Romans drove them back. It was a trap of their own making. Around seventy thousand Brits and their sympathizers died while only four hundred Romans were killed (according to the Romans).

Watling Street was one of the key battles that changed the future of Britannia forever. The rebellion had come close to success. Roman Emperor Nero, no hero, seriously considered abandoning Britain. Then the famous fiddler heard of Paulinus' success at Watling Street and changed his mind. The Brits had learnt their lesson and paid the price with around 350 more years of Roman rule.

As for Boudicca, she is thought to have poisoned herself to avoid capture. The exact site of the battle, and of Boudicca's death, are unknown, but some observers place Boudicca's buried bones under Platform 8 at Kings Cross Station. (Some modern commuters also consider poisoning themselves there rather than waiting for a British train.) What is certain is that, for Boudicca and the rebels, it was quite simply the end of the woad.

The people of northern Britain, the Picts, were never subdued. Living in the region we now call Scotland, the Picts were tougher opponents than the softer southerners. They never engaged in a pitched battle but fought an effective guerrilla campaign whenever the Roman legions approached. Then they raided the southern Britons who, naturally, turned to their Roman overlords for protection.

The early Picts may have called themselves Cruithne – 'wheat-growers' – but the Romans came along and changed all that. They called them the 'Picts' and the name stuck like cold haggis on the roof of your mouth. 'Pict' could be the Roman word for 'painter' or 'painted'. This gives clever historians the chance to argue why the Romans gave them this name. Maybe they were called Painted People because they covered themselves with tattoos, or maybe they couldn't write so they carved stones with pictures and were the Picture People. Maybe the bright tartan clothes they wore made them Painted Cloth People, or they went into battle wearing blue woad and no clothes.* Painted people or painted cloth? What's the truth? Take your Pict.

If you think the name 'Pict' is peculiar, then the name 'Scot' is even more weird. According to legend, it comes from Egypt . . .

Just before AD 500, Fergus MacErc and his five Gaelic brothers came from Ireland. They took over a Pict area and called their kingdom Dalriada, after their homeland. In the distant mists of time, one of those early MacErc ancestors had married a Pharaoh's daughter in Egypt and brought her back to Ireland. Her name was Scota. She brought some unusual luggage with her. In the Bible there's a story of Jacob falling asleep with his head on a pillow of stone. Scota brought this stone with her from Egypt, and Fergus, who eventually inherited it, took it across to Pictland. Now known as the 'Stone of Destiny', it was pinched by Edward I in 1296 and used as an English coronation stone for

---

* The earliest evidence of tartan is from the AD 200s. A small piece of tartan fabric was found used as a stopper for a pot which contained silver coins.

centuries until, in 1996, it was returned to Scotland. To be really fair, the Scots should now send it back to Egypt, so Jacob can get a decent night's sleep. (Bet they don't.)

The Romans never managed to conquer Pictland, but they did bring all the Pict tribes together. The tribes forgot their squabbles among each other to face the invading Romans and, unlike the Britons in the south, they never made peace.

They didn't always win their battles for freedom. At the Battle of Mons Graupius in AD 84 the Picts lost. The Romans burnt Pict homes and drove the surviving warriors into the mountains. That's when the Pict leader Calgacus made one of those famous speeches that have gone down in history. He summed up the Roman Empire very shrewdly. While historians down the ages have called the Romans 'civilized', Calgacus said they were 'robbers of the world. Having exhausted the land, they rifle the deep. If the enemy be rich, they are rapacious; if their enemy be poor, they lust for dominion; neither the east nor the west has been able to satisfy them. Alone among men they covet with equal eagerness poverty and riches. To robbery, slaughter, plunder, they give the lying name of empire; they make a desert and call it peace.'*

In the interest of balance, I must say that the Scottish tribes have their critics too. One tribe, the Attacotti, scared the Romans more than any other. Nowadays, we'd describe them as Glaswegians. St Jerome wrote (around 410) of a fearless tribe of Scotland

---

* Great stuff, Calgacus . . . though it's probable that the fiery speech was made up by the eloquent Tacitus. In fact, some historians say Tacitus even invented Calgacus himself.

who enjoyed the taste of human flesh. He said: 'On a visit to Gaul, I heard that the Attacotti, a British tribe, eat human flesh, and that although they find herds of swine, and droves of large or small cattle in the woods, it is their custom to cut off the buttocks of the shepherds and the breasts of their women, and to regard them as the greatest delicacies.' And Jerome is a saint, so he wouldn't lie, would he? Equally, the monk and chronicler Gildas (500–570) summed up the Pict people: 'The Picts and Scots are wandering thieves who have no taste for war. They are allies because they both share their greed for bloodshed.'

The Scottish tribes were never suppressed for long. Just two years after winning at Mons Graupius, the Romans packed their bags and left the Picts in peace. (There was trouble over in Romania and they couldn't spare the troops.) Four decades later, in AD 120, Emperor Hadrian had the idea to build a wall to keep out illegal immigrants. It was less than 90 miles long but was up to 15 feet high which, given the technology of the day, was impressive. As Hadrian might have said, 'Right, lads, the Roman Empire stops here. Let the Picts have their rotten Caledonia.' (Except in Latin.)

Around 410 the Romans would return home to Italy, but the Italian influence was far from over. Britannia had converted to the new Roman religion, Christianity. And where was the top man who told all good British Christians what to do? In Rome, of course. The called him Father or, in their quaint language, *Papa*.

The Roman Empire had departed Britain, leaving very little behind apart from the odd straight road and bits of walls that would give archaeologists a meagre living for a millennium and a half. They came back in an unexpected way, as the Catholic Church. This was the ultimate irony because the ancient Romans had tortured and killed Christians for sport.

Emperor Nero had initially used the radical new Jewish sect as scapegoats for the Great Fire of Rome. He covered them in animal skins to be torn apart by packs of hungry dogs. Other unfortunate victims were tied to poles, covered in tar and set alight to illuminate Nero's public gardens. Incidentally, this is said to be the origin of the fireworks called 'Roman candles'. Catherine wheels refer to St Catherine, who was never actually tied to a flaming wheel. She had converted the wife of Emperor Maxentius and was sent to be 'broken' on a wheel. The wheel itself broke – a miracle! – so she was beheaded instead.

When Nero died, the violence against the Christians subsided, but it continued to flare intermittently over the following centuries across the empire. A famine here or an earthquake there? Blame the Christians.

Emperor Trajan, who ruled from AD 98 to 117, received a letter from magistrate Pliny (the Younger one, AD 61–112) asking how to deal with a rash of complaints against Christians. A lot of reports were obviously from spiteful neighbours and Pliny thought he couldn't execute them all. He suggested compelling them to sacrifice to the Roman gods, declare loyalty to Emperor Trajan and curse the name of Christ. Trajan's decision was to declare Christianity illegal. Members of the faith were not to be sought out; but if they were accused and convicted, they must be punished.

So, no witch-hunt, but execute them if you can't ignore the

complaints. That said, there were localized persecutions in places like Lyons in AD 177. The Lyons martyrs were arrested and tortured. A typical feature of any persecution was the way the victims were betrayed. Servants who were arrested feared execution, so they pointed the finger at their masters. The persecuted martyrs included Blandina. A frail lady, her fellow Christians said, yet she stood up to torture so resolutely that her torturers were exhausted. As a non-Roman citizen she didn't enjoy the (relative) privilege of being beheaded. Instead she was tied to a stake and wild beasts were set on her. They didn't so much as nibble her. Finally, she was whipped, dropped on a red-hot grate, wrapped in a net and thrown to a wild bull who tossed her into the air. When she landed, she was finished off with a dagger.

The Roman persecutors claimed that the Christians buried their dead in corridors under the ground – catacombs – and that they drank the blood of their Jesus in their services – but of course it couldn't really have been *His* blood. The Roman extremists reasoned that the Christians must be murdering children and drinking their blood instead. They were cannibals and deserved to die.

Books have been filled with the persecutions. These stories were so horrific that, over time, they elicited sympathy rather than hatred. In a seismic transformation, Rome became the heart of the Christian religion. By 300, Christianity had taken over as the dominant religion in many parts of the empire, due mainly to the missionary work of early Christians.

Then, around 312, Constantine the Great became a patron of Christianity. This gave Christianity a great deal of political and social influence and made it more attractive to potential converts.

If you wanted to advance in the world then you joined the dominant sect. That sect didn't have to involve a funny handshake. You simply made the sign of the Cross or swore, 'by Christ' or 'by Jesus, Mary, Joseph and the wee donkey'.

Christianity became the official religion of the empire and led to the establishment of state-supported churches. The Romans, being Romans, made sure control stayed in Rome. From being the city of 'I'm a Christian, get me out of here', it became the Holy City. And the big-cheese bishop of the religion would reside in his own enclave within the city – the Vatican.

By the second millennium, the popes had become the undisputed leaders of the Western Church. (The Greek speakers in the Eastern Empire decided to do their own thing.) The popes had the power to appoint bishops and excommunicate heretics. That power extended to Britain. It united Britain to a large extent, so long as everyone went along with the superstition that the pope in Rome was God's infallible representative on Earth. The monarchs in Britain went along with it as the pope's infallible representatives on the islands of Britannia.

Now the Brits wouldn't mind so much if the popes were useful – opening doors to heaven for righteous people (like you and me) and a trapdoor direct to hell for traffic wardens, spammers and next-door's cat. But they weren't. They were holy men; they were not wholly good.

The British people paid their tithes – a tenth of their income – to the priests, who passed on a share to feed the fantasies, feastings and fatness of the popes, most of whom probably couldn't point to Britain on a map. If the peasants didn't like it they could revolt against the Church, but they faced excommunication and a miserable eternal afterlife. And still, up to fifty years ago, historians like Kenneth Clark (1903–83) were proclaiming that 'the great achievement of the Catholic Church lay in harmonizing, civilizing the deepest impulses of ordinary, ignorant people'. (Incidentally, Ken died a Catholic.)

Even though a historian said it, we might want to question how far the Roman Church 'harmonized' the 'ignorant' British. Henry I (1068–1135) wanted to appoint his own bishops and the pope in Rome was furious. A compromise was reached in 1107 with the Concordat of London, which gave the king the right to appoint bishops – as long as they were approved by the pope. According to this one-sided agreement, the pope still had the right to appoint a British bishop without the British monarch's agreement.

When King John (1166–1216) refused to accept Stephen Langton as archbishop of Canterbury, Pope Innocent III decreed in the Interdict of 1208 that all religious services were suspended. Innocent's order made an exception for baptism of the young, and confessions and absolutions for the dying. It deteriorated into a petty tit-for-tat squabble. Tit: John seized Church lands and the prostitutes the priests kept. (Nice touch that one, John. Hit them where it hurts.) Tat: Innocent III excommunicated John so he couldn't get into heaven when he died. The interdict was lifted in 1214 after John agreed to become the pope's vassal.

Naturally, the recording of John's misdeeds came mainly from the Catholic monks and his reward was to be recorded as the second-most reviled English king after the child-murdering Richard III. Matthew of Paris (1200–59), a Benedictine monk and English chronicler, didn't even give bad King John a break after he had died: 'Foul as it is, hell itself is made fouler by the presence of King John.' Matt suggested that King John had gone to the emir of Morocco with a deal: help me fight my enemies and I'll turn England into a Muslim country. Do we scent bias there? No, more likely downright lies.

We do know that John was struggling to implement a form of breakaway from the Church in Rome (Chexit?). What's interesting is how differently historians report John's alleged crimes.

Catholic history says John killed his father, Henry II. Dad loved John more than any of his brothers, but John betrayed him. Henry, on his deathbed, heard that John wasn't just *one* of the conspirators against him . . . he was the *first*. Henry, it was said, died from grief.

British history says all of Henry's sons rebelled against their father, who was vicious. For example, Henry II took twenty-two hostages from the Welsh in 1165, ordered that the men be blinded and castrated and that the women should have their noses and ears cut off.

Catholic history says that John's older brother, Richard I, went off on a crusade and not only banned John from entering Britain to snatch the crown, but nominated his nephew Arthur to succeed him in the event of his dying in the Holy Land. Young Arthur went to Uncle John for protection but John imprisoned Arthur and ordered his jailers to kill him. They refused. What happened next was brutal, according to the monkish chronicler: 'After King John had captured Arthur and kept him alive in prison for some time, at length, in the castle of Rouen, after dinner on the Thursday before Easter, when he was drunk and possessed by the devil, he slew him with his own hand, and tying a heavy stone to the body cast it into the Seine. It was discovered by a fisherman in his net, and being dragged to the bank and recognized, was taken for secret burial, in fear of the tyrant.'

British history says that the evidence that John murdered his nephew is ambiguous, and claims that Arthur (a sixteen-year-old boy) had put himself at the head of a rebellion sponsored by Philip Augustus of France.

Catholic history says that in 1208 King John told Matilda of Hay to send her son William as a hostage to make sure his Welsh enemies behaved themselves. Matilda refused, and she rashly called him Arthur's murderer. John's retaliation was to have Matilda and son walled up alive in a cell at Windsor Castle with just a piece of raw bacon and a sheaf of wheat. They were both found dead after eleven days. So desperate was Matilda that she had eaten her son's cheeks.

Britannia says you can't prove that John gave the order.

Catholic history says that John was greedy for land but not very brave in snatching it from his enemies. There were reports of him running away from a battle – often disguised as a woman. Britannia says that while, yes, John did avoid open battles, most rulers of the time did the same. John was actually very good at sieges, you know.

Catholic history says that John took Welsh hostages numbering twenty-eight boys – the children of treacherous families – to his castle in Nottingham. One young hostage, the son of a troublemaker called Maelgwn, was just seven years old. When news arrived of another Welsh revolt, John's jailers put ropes round the boys' necks. (It didn't hurt them.) They were made to climb to the top of a high wall. (That didn't hurt them either.)

Maelgwn's little boy was crying. The guards secured the ropes then pushed the boys off the ramparts. (Now that would have hurt a bit, I imagine.) They kicked and struggled because the youngest boys didn't have the weight to snap their own necks in a clean and quick death.

Britannia respectfully points out that an earlier king, Stephen, had been derided because he *didn't* execute a child hostage and was mocked as 'weak'.

Catholic history says John was nicknamed Lackland because he struggled to hang on to the traditional family lands in France as well as England.* He ended up losing both.

Well, Shakespeare didn't mention that the old English Channel – that moat 'against the envy of less happier lands' – worked both ways. It meant the Brits *inside* the moat struggled to get out to attack their European neighbours. John was hampered by rebel barons too – an enemy within as well as the French enemies without.

Britannia's verdict? John was no better or worse than most medieval monarchs. He just upset the media.

Should Britannia have simply submitted to Pope Innocent III anyway, to keep the peace? When rebel Cathars in France defied Innocent III, the pope sent in a Catholic army to butcher them into line. Arnaud Amalric, the pope's Cistercian abbot-commander, told the troops to spare no one and not to let it bother their tender consciences. 'Kill them all; the Lord will recognize His own.' Thousands were mutilated and killed. Prisoners were

---

* His other nickname was Soft-Sword, but it's not what you're thinking – it was because he wasn't keen on tackling armed knights.

blinded, dragged behind horses and used for target practice. What remained of the city was burnt to the ground. Pope Innocent III? Pope Guilty more like.

This was the vicious Roman pope that John was trying to save his country from. Good King John, hero of Britannia.

In October 1216 John died. Just as no one could agree about his life, no one could agree about what killed him. Conflicting reports blame being killed by poisoned ale, poisoned plums or a 'surfeit of peaches'.

As well as being one of Britain's most maligned monarchs, King John is remembered for the Myth of Magna Carta, the document that is often said to mark the beginning of British democracy (when it was simply a peace treaty between John and his disgruntled barons). One of those icons of British specialness that patriots love to point at. The British comedian Tony Hancock (1924–68) parodied it best in an episode of his comedy series. 'Does Magna Carta mean nothing to you? Did she die in vain? That brave Hungarian peasant girl who forced King John to sign the pledge at Runnymede and close the boozers at half past ten? Is all this to be forgotten?'

In fact, the pope was the big winner. Clause 1 of Magna Carta promises: 'The English Church shall be free and enjoy her rights in their integrity and her liberties untouched.' Sounds reasonable. Except it never was an 'English' Church – it was the Roman Church. The message was, 'King John, butt out of the pope's business.' In any event, John ratted on the agreement at the first opportunity.

John is remembered for tearing up Magna Carta (even though it was the pope that did it). The barons were worse than John:

they invited Prince Louis of France to invade and take Rochester Castle – which he did. Pure treason. And they say John was bad.

Three hundred years after John lost his battle with Innocent III, the popes were still controlling the hearts and minds of British people through their priests. Discontent was growing across the western world at the Roman stranglehold. Protestants were protesting. But in southern Britain the pope had a defender of the faith (who was incidentally also one of the most monstrous, murdering psychopaths in history): Henry VIII.

Many history books have told the simple story – because we general readers are seen as simple people: 'In 1527, Henry VIII wanted a divorce from Catherine of Aragon because she couldn't deliver him a son. The pope refused to grant the divorce, so Henry divorced the Catholic Church, created the Church of England, and granted himself his own divorce.'

It's simple and memorable. A wicked man does something good for selfish reasons. But there is another side to the story. Henry wasn't the only one complaining about the institutions of Catholicism. There were many 'people of good conscience' around Europe rising up against rule from the Vatican, as the papacy sank into a cesspit of corruption and abuse of power. Back when the English civil war of 1139–54 was brewing the *Laud (Peterborough) Chronicle* raged: 'And men said openly that Christ and His saints slept.' If they were asleep in the 1100s, in the later Middle Ages Christ, God, the angels and the little baby cherubs must have been comatose. Look at what they allowed their Roman representatives on Earth to get away with.

Dietrich Urach (b. 1420), a German poet, wrote: 'The Pope,

once the wonder of the world, has fallen. Then came the age of clay. Could aught be worse? Aye, dung, and in dung sits the papal court.' The movement that became known as Protestantism had been brewing for more than a hundred years before Henry VIII joined the tide that was ebbing away from the Vatican. The question is *not* 'Why did Henry abandon the Catholic Church?' The question is 'What took him so long?'

By the Renaissance any pope would be conflicted – he had his sacred duties, but he also had earthly estates to attend to. Heaven or Earth? The earthly began to win.

Alexander VI (1431–1503) was born as Rodrigo Borgia in Spain and was elected pope in 1492. Rumour had it he spent a fortune on bribing the right cardinals to vote for him and to lobby others. Alex loved the good life – or rather the 'bad' life, if you were a pope. He was father to at least twelve children through a number of mistresses. It is said that under Alex's rule, his Borgia family hosted orgies in the Vatican palace. Their 'Banquet of Chestnuts' was (allegedly) an extravagant and scandalous gathering which took place in 1501. It was said to have involved fifty sex workers (or 'honest prostitutes', as the master of ceremonies Johann Burchard described them). They gradually stripped down to their bare skin and engaged in suggestive games involving chestnuts. (Use your imagination here.) The male guests were scored according to how often they 'performed' and prizes were awarded. Their hosts were the Borgia family, including Pope Alexander VI, his son Cesare and his daughter Lucrezia. Chestnuts have become the symbol of the family's decadence.

Alex's most notorious son Cesare acquired a reputation for the murder of political rivals. Lucrezia was married off to a number of husbands one after another for political gain. When Lucrezia's lover made her pregnant at an awkward time, he ended up in the River Tiber. Pope Alex said the child was his. Incest? As the British conductor Thomas Beecham (1879–1961) (allegedly) said: 'Try everything once except incest and folk dancing.'

Never mind. Rival families who tried to usurp his power were dealt with by Borgia brutality. Members of the rival Orsini clan were thrown into dungeons where the men could be quietly strangled.

For all his family inheritance, Alex VI always needed money. The piggy bank wasn't an option – he chose wars for conquest and loot. He sold high Church appointments – you could almost call that a cardinal sin. He raised money with the sale of 'indulgences', written proclamations that forgave you your trespasses when you got to heaven's door. Wave the indulgence under St Peter's nose and walk straight in. You could even be forgiven for crimes before you commit them. Want to rob a bank? Alex needs his cut.

Alex died of bodily corruption. His stomach became swollen and turned to liquid. His bowels bled copiously, which seems to suggest his diet contained poison. Don Cesare, Alex's illegitimate son, sent a gang to strip the papal palace of all its treasures. When they found a cardinal in residence they threatened to cut his throat and throw him out of the window. The pope's corpse was laid out in a chapel where its face turned wine-coloured and the skin began to peel off. Johann Burchard said the nose was swollen, the mouth distended where the tongue was doubled over, and the lips seemed to fill everything. The appearance of the face then was far more horrifying than anything that had ever been seen or reported before.

Labourers made crude jokes as they stuffed Alex's bloated body into a coffin that was too small. Burchard went on: 'They placed the pope's mitre at his side, rolled his body up in an old carpet, and pummelled and pushed it into the coffin with their fists.' Live like a gangster, die rolled up in a carpet.

Henry VIII was crowned in 1509 and was soon under the papal power of Leo X (pope from 1513 to 1521). The Italian Leo entered the ranks of the Roman Catholic clergy at the age of seven and was made a cardinal by Pope Innocent VIII at thirteen. At the age of eighteen he opposed the appointment of Alexander VI, then very wisely fled Rome before the pope took revenge. When Alex died, Leo worked for his successor, Julius II. Leo took the hot seat – or throne – at the age of thirty-seven.

Just as a British political party can fill the House of Lords with appointed peers, Leo filled posts with his family. Of the thirty-seven cardinal jobs going, how many went to Leo's relatives? Thirty-seven, of course. But Leo was unloved, and his minions uncovered a plot to assassinate him. An enemy cardinal was executed. It would never do for a pope to order the death of a cardinal, so the plotter perished from 'food poisoning'. Maybe he ordered the same thing Alexander VI did.

Leo welcomed and gave financial support to writers. Clearly a top bloke and one of the best popes ever. When he became pope, Leo X allegedly said: 'Since God has given us the papacy, let us enjoy it.' God didn't argue, so She must have approved. Leo then broke the papal bank to spend heavily on fine clothes and jewellery, extravagant feasts and parties. He also patronized artists such as Michelangelo, Raphael and Leonardo da Vinci, so it wasn't all waste. He returned to the old scam of selling indulgences. This was the final straw for a young monk who, on 31 October 1517, nailed a long list of grievances to the door of a church in Germany. His name was Martin Luther (1483–1546) and this act launched the Protestant Reformation. He proclaimed his Ninety-five Theses in opposition to many of the Church's practices. Leo retorted: 'He's a drunken German who will soon be sober.' Ominous.

In 1521, with Henry VIII's help, Leo drove the French from Italy. That earned Henry the ultimate Brownie Point, the title 'Defender of the Faith'. In Henry's little mind it also meant that the papacy owed him. It would not be long before the Tudor would be seeking papal payback. Henry must have assumed that the popes were in his pocket. (Or codpiece? Doesn't bear thinking about.)

Leo died suddenly not long after — probably something he ate. By 1523 one of his cousins became Pope Clement VII and Henry asked for a simple divorce from his queen, Catherine of Aragon. Clement said 'No,' pointing out that Catherine was the aunt of Holy Roman Emperor Charles V, a powerful enemy of the papacy. Allowing Auntie Catherine to be cast aside as Queen of England could have tipped Charles V into all-out war against the pope. Second, Clement VII was also worried about the precedent that an annulment for Henry would set.

The popes were fellow princes as much as they were men of God. Clement VII eventually ruled in March 1534 that Henry's 1533 marriage to Anne Boleyn was invalid and adulterous. Henry was so aggrieved that he decided to set up his own Church, the Church of England. He would be its head and grant himself a divorce. Henry's actual words were: 'We are, by the sufferance of God, King of England; and the Kings of England in times past never had any superior but God.'* In November 1534, Parliament passed an Act that stated that Henry VIII was now the head of the Church of England.

After breaking away from the Catholic Church, Henry VIII continued to use the title 'Defender of the Faith'. However, he now used it to defend the Church of England from Catholic attacks.

Henry did for Britain what John had failed to do. He snapped the chain that the Romans had wrapped around the people of Britain. But far from uniting southern Britons into a front against Roman authority, it split the nation to this day. Catholics and Protestants burnt, hanged, tortured, shot and persecuted one another. Britain had also made a major step away from integration into Europe.

Thanks, Rome. Thanks, Henry. You never saw that coming, did you?

---

* King John's ghost must have been cheering, 'That's what I was saying three hundred years ago. Way to go, Henry . . . just go easy on the peaches.'

2
SAXONY

The Saxons (and their neighbours the Angles) came from the area we now call northern Germany and southern Denmark. Some historians argue that they were two separate peoples, while others insist that they were one people divided into two groups. If you were a Briton in the AD 400s, it's not the sort of thing you would think to question as you ran for your life.

The English crime writer Dorothy L. Sayers (1893–1957) once said: 'Death seems to provide the minds of the Anglo-Saxon race with a greater fund of amusement than any other single subject.' Those Angle and Saxon invaders must have been laughing all the way to the graveyards. And if the Germans of the twentieth century gave Britons a sense of unity, the Angles gave southern Britain a name – Angle-land.

They had a major influence on English, which became the principal language of the British Isles. Celtic languages are still spoken in Scotland, Ireland, Wales and Brittany by one to two million people. Surprisingly, there are very few Celtic words left in the English language. There are ones like *cross, crag, bin* and *brock* (for badger) and some place names like the rivers *Thames*,

Avon and *Exe*, the county of *Kent* and the town of *Dover*. But much of the rest is Anglo-Saxon mixed with French.

Around 410 the Romans had abandoned Britain as they pulled back their armies to fight in defence of the homeland. It left the tribes of southern Britain without an identity. The inhabitants of Britannia were no longer Roman, but for three centuries they lacked strong, independent tribes. This power vacuum was partially filled by a British king: Vortigern.

Gildas tells us how the Saxons arrived. Gildas was contemptuous of Vortigern, so he could be exaggerating the miserable monarch's incompetence, cowardice and sheer stupidity. But according to the story, the Picts and Scots were up to their old tricks, attacking the former Roman territory south of the border along Hadrian's defunct Wall. Vortigern had no effective standing army to defend the south of Britain. He needed mercenaries. So Vortigern invited some warriors over from Saxony to fight his battles. They were led by brothers Hengist and Horsa from Jutland, now part of Denmark.

This account comes with a disclaimer: we need to remember that the story of Hengist and Horsa is likely to be a mixture of fact and fiction. There is no archaeological evidence to support the claim that Hengist and Horsa were real people. The story of their invasion of Britain may have been exaggerated over time. And that's a huge shame, because it is a great tale of hubris and betrayal. But let's tell the story that British schoolchildren have been told for a thousand years, since it has become as much part of the national memory as the Battle of Hastings and Braveheart and Anne Boleyn's walking the Tower of London with her head tucked underneath her arm.

Hengist and Horsa landed in Kent in 449 with a small band of warriors. They quickly defeated the Picts and Scots, and Vortigern rewarded them with land at Thanet in Kent. Gildas wrote: 'A small group of the fierce and impious Saxons first landed on the eastern side of the island, by the invitation of the unlucky tyrant, and there fixed their sharp talons, apparently to fight in favour of the island but, alas, more truly against it.'

If Gildas was a critic of Vortigern, then the chronicler William of Malmesbury (1080–1143) was positively defamatory: 'At this time Vortigern was king of Britain; a man calculated neither for the field nor the council, but wholly given up to the lusts of the flesh, the slave of every vice: a character of insatiable avarice, ungovernable pride, and polluted by his lusts. To complete the picture ... he had defiled his own daughter, who was lured to the participation of such a crime by the hope of sharing his kingdom, and she had borne him a son.' Another historical character accused of incest. At least he hasn't been tainted with accusations of folk dancing.

Hengist and Horsa apparently sussed Vortigern's lusts and offered Hengist's daughter, Rowena, in marriage. Rowena's opinion is not recorded and was probably not sought. Or she could have been part of the conspiracy. As for Vortigern, we can only assume the sick man had grown tired of his own daughter. Vortigern's son, Vortimer, was suspicious, and accused the Saxon mercenaries of plotting to overthrow the king. But Vortigern refused to listen to his son's warnings, an ancient failing summed up by the phrase 'There's no fool like an old fool'.

Vortigern married Rowena. In exchange for her hand he let her brothers expand their lands from Thanet to the whole of

Kent. The Saxons made themselves at home and liked it, so they invited their fierce and impious mates to join them.

The mercenaries increased their demands for payment, and when they weren't met they began to plunder their Romano-British neighbours. Vortigern found he had a backbone after all and fought back and Hengist suggested a peace conference on Salisbury Plain. Only a mug would go to meet an enemy unarmed. Vortigern was a mug. What happened next became known as 'The Night of the Long Knives' ... so you can guess what's coming.

We know about the Night of the Long Knives from the *Anglo-Saxon Chronicle*, an anonymous collection of historical writings from the 800s. It is one of the most important sources of information about Anglo-Saxon England. It's a year-by-year account of events in England from the arrival of Hengist and Horsa in 449 to the year 1154. It is pretty clearly biased towards the West Saxon kingdom and often omits or downplays events that didn't affect the West Saxons. To be honest, the *Chronicle* is not always accurate. It contains folk tales, legends and outright factual errors. Bearing that in mind, the *Chronicle* said:

> And Hengist ordered the whole of his household that each one should hide his knife under his foot in the middle of his shoe. 'And when I shall call out to you and say, "Draw your swords", then draw your knives from the soles of your shoes, and fall upon them, and stand strongly against them. And do not kill their king but seize him for the sake of my daughter whom I gave to him in matrimony, because it is better for us that he should be ransomed from our hands.' And they brought

together the conference, and the Saxons, speaking in a friendly way, meanwhile were thinking in a wolvish way, and sociably they sat down man beside man. Hengist, as he had said, spoke out, and all the three hundred elders of King Vortigern were slaughtered, and only he was imprisoned, and was chained, and he gave to them many regions for the ransom of his soul.

Over the next few centuries, the Anglo-Saxons continued to emigrate from northern Germany to Britain and conquer more land. By the seventh century they had established seven kingdoms in England: Northumbria, Mercia, Wessex, East Anglia, Essex, Kent and Sussex. Coming over here, naming our counties.

It is odd that Vortigern is treated as a myth while Arthur – on far less evidence – is revered by some as a real-life national hero. According to this definitely-not-made-up account, Merlin joined Arthur to weave his magic and together they led the old Brits' resistance movement in a series of battles, plotting their strategies to fight off dragons and giants at the famous Round Table. After his last battle, Arthur and his knights retired to an underground cave to sleep. They would awaken in Britain's hour of greatest need and drive off the invaders.*

We can be fairly sure that the Britons who weren't integrated

---

* Maybe Arthur forgot to set his alarm clock because they didn't emerge from their slumbers when the Vikings arrived, or when William the Conqueror landed at Hastings. And where were they when the Saxons' descendants – the Luftwaffe – arrived to bomb old King Lud's resting place?

into these new Saxon territories retreated to the mountains of Wales in the west or crossed the sea to settle in Ireland. Old Britain simply wasn't united enough to organize a resistance, so the Saxons edged north till they stopped around Hadrian's deserted Wall – afraid, like almost everyone, of the painted men in kilts. Then something did happen to unify the seven kingdoms: Christianity.

The historian Bede (d. 735) told the story of Pope Gregory the Great (pope from 590 to 604). Greg the Great saw some Anglo-Saxon boys being badly treated in a Roman slave market. He was told they were Angles and cried: *'Non Angli, sed angeli.'* Not Angles, but angels. In Latin or English, it still doesn't get into the Top Ten of All-Time Great Jokes. It may even be apocryphal. But it *has* been remembered after fourteen hundred years and that's quite an achievement.

Pope Gregory promptly sent Augustine, prior of a monastery in Rome, to become St Augustine of Canterbury, along with forty other missionaries. In 597 all the Anglo-Saxon kingdom had been pagan. St Augustine landed in King Æthelbert's kingdom of Kent and Æthelbert said, 'I shall not harm you,' which was pretty hospitable of him, for a Saxon.

King Æthelbert not only made St Gus welcome but had himself and most of his people converted to Christianity. This was the first ever Christian kingdom in England, so Æth became a saint. You will notice that Æthelbert, being posh, didn't have to starve or suffer a horrible death like so many early saints. Even you could be a saint if it were usually that easy. Just say to that traffic warden, 'I shall not harm you.' Bingo. Arise, St Reader.

It's harder to understand why Augustine became a saint. He

converted Brits using threats and massacres. But remember, those Celtic refugees in Wales saw themselves as different. They would be the first to break the harmony of a united Christian country.

In 606 the Welsh Christians had a falling out with the pope, because they didn't worship the same way as the Saxon Christians. The Welsh worshipped different saints, celebrated Easter at a different time, baptized people by dunking the whole person in the water and – most important – had different haircuts. The Welsh monks shaved the entire front of the head from ear to ear, while the Saxon monks left a ring of hair round the head. (They probably agreed that mullets were ungodly.) Bangor Monastery had 2,400 monks. Taking it in turns, they made sure that a hundred monks were singing each hour of the day, which must have made sleeping a bit difficult.

Augustine said the Welsh Christians should meet him and talk about the problem. They agreed to assemble at an oak tree. St Dinas from Bangor-Iscoed Monastery set off to join him. A wise man had told Dinas: 'Let Augustine get to the meeting place first. He'll sit in his chair. Walk up to him. If he stands up to greet you he is a humble man. Obey him. And if he remains seated he is a proud man. Do not obey him.' Simple.

Of course, Augustine didn't stand up. So the Welsh refused to take his orders. Augustine said God would destroy Dinas and his monastery. (Well, God with a little earthly help.) Augustine raged, 'If the Welsh will not have peace with us, they shall die at the hands of the Saxons.'

Augustine then went to the Saxon King Æthelfrith of Bernicia in the north and made a suggestion. Why not attack Chester?

And since the monastery at Bangor was only about twelve miles south of Chester, it might be a good idea to attack that while you're there.

Æthelfrith set off to attack Chester. A messenger intercepted him to beg for peace. The messenger was sent back to Chester . . . in a box . . . chopped into little pieces. Æthelfrith attacked Chester, then turned on the monastery. Hundreds of monks were murdered. Only fifty lived to chant the tale.* So much for loving your neighbour.

If a nation is unified by its enemies, then the Welsh learnt very early in their history to distrust the Saxons. They are also united and divided by a common language. In 1965, the Welsh Language Society (Cymdeithas yr Iaith Gymraeg) began a campaign for bilingual road signs. They argued that Welsh speakers had a right to see their language displayed in public places. It took until 1983 for bilingual signs to become a legal requirement. Since then, all new road signs in Wales have been bilingual, with Welsh appearing first. So Welsh speakers are united by a common enemy – not just the Saxons to the east, but the English-speaking Welsh to the south. These days, murdered monks matter less than road signs.

As for the Anglo-Saxons, despite bringing their kingdoms together in Christianity, their rule would fail to unite Britannia when invaders threatened – first the Vikings from Scandinavia and then their cousins from northern France, the Normans, who made the Saxons their serfs. More of them later.

---

* Of course, some Christians say Augustine did not have the monks murdered because he died in 605, around ten years before the Battle of Chester.

3
SCANDINAVIA

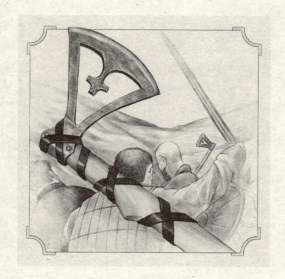

Denmark, Sweden and Norway are historically associated with the Vikings. They are best known as pillagers of villagers in Britannia. Yet it was a Scandinavian king who united England into a single kingdom.

Like most big groups of people, the Scandinavians of our imaginations are a myth. They aren't mostly blond, IKEA-shopping, ABBA-singing Volvo drivers who weekend in their longboat on a fjord. But monks at the time of the Viking invaders did stereotype them under the name 'Northmen' as they prayed for their God to protect them from the savage Scandinavian sailors.

A furore Normannorum libera nos, Domine.

They seemed to assume their Lord spoke Latin. If She didn't, then they could have tried English:

From the fury of the Northmen, deliver us, O Lord.

Apart from the occasional St Augustine-inspired massacre, the Anglo-Saxon monks lived fairly peacefully, writing scripts in their scriptoriums, growing vegetables on their allotments and at least vaguely sticking to rules of poverty, chastity and obedience.

They certainly suffered for their quiet lives. The abbot of Monkwearmouth, a monastery in north-eastern England, wrote in a letter to a friend in Germany: 'During the past winter our island has been savagely troubled with cold and ice and with long and widespread storms of wind and rain. It is so bad that the hands of the writers become numb and cannot produce a very large number of books.'

Not all the monks were poor or chaste or obedient. So the first raids of the Vikings were seen by many goody-goody monks as a divine retribution for the bad ones. Saxon letters have survived with complaints like this one: 'My dear abbess, I was shocked and horrified on my visit to your convent. I expected to see holy women, simply and modestly dressed. What did I find? Nuns who crimped their hair with curling irons; nuns wearing brightly coloured headdresses laced with ribbons down to their ankles; nuns who sharpened their fingernails like hawks. I hope these disgraceful practices will cease immediately.'

Many monks were no better. The monk-historian Bede told the story of Coldingham Monastery in Northumbria: 'The cells that were built for praying were turned into places of feasting and drinking.' A Celt called Adamnan warned that he had a dream in which he saw the monastery destroyed. The Coldingham monks behaved themselves for a while after Adamnan's warning. Then they went back to their old ways and the monastery was destroyed by fire in 679. Bede said the fire was God's punishment.*

A DNA Survey for *The Daily Telegraph* in July 2016 calculated:

> The average British resident . . . is 36.94 per cent Anglo-Saxon, 21.59 per cent Celtic and 19.91 per cent Western European, from regions in France and Germany. Another 9.2 per cent of an average Briton is originally from Scandinavia.

So it seems the British are a mongrel race.† Under 2 per cent of British genes are from Italy or Greece, so those old Romans clearly didn't spend a lot of time fraternizing with the natives. By contrast, nearly 10 per cent of modern British genes are from Scandinavia. Obviously, those Vikings had a lot to answer for.

The monks were no better when it came to recklessly splashing their DNA around. In 734 Bede himself took time off from his historical parchments to write to the bishop of York, complaining: 'Your Grace, As you are aware a monk vows to lead a

---

* If it seems shocking to think that people in holy orders used to use their status to cover their illicit behaviour, we should cast our minds back to 2015, when former bishop Peter Ball, once friend of Prince Charles and some Cabinet ministers, was jailed for the sex abuse of teenagers and young men. Ball had been cautioned by police as far back as 1993 for gross indecency.
† I said 'mongrel', not Mongol. Mind you, I have met quite a few people who could safely claim to be descended from Genghis Khan. Nightclub doormen and PE teachers mostly.

single life, without the company of women. I was disgusted to note that monks in one of your monasteries were not only married – they were living in the monastery with their wives and children.' Bede also whinged about priests. They were guilty of 'laughter, jokes, stories, feasting and drunkenness'. Bede was not someone you'd want at your office Christmas party.

Even a strict monastery, like Bede's own Monkwearmouth, had problems with boys who preferred playing to praying. Just fifty years after Bede's death, a monk named Alcuin was complaining that young monks at Monkwearmouth were having a wild time hunting foxes and hares: 'How wicked to leave the service of Christ for a fox hunt.' He was a real killjoy and raged against the rich lords and the poverty they caused:

> Look at the immoderate use of clothes, beyond any necessity of human nature. This superfluity of the princes is the poverty of the people. Some are loaded with garments, while others perish with cold. Some flow over with luxuries and feasts like the rich man in purple, while Lazarus at the gate dies of hunger.

Making an argument not far off the original 1917 Labour constitution, Alcuin was sure that God would sort out the poverty gap if the rich didn't do it themselves. In those days, divine justice came in the form of aggressive, hairy men with longboats, axes and swords.

The Saxons couldn't complain. They'd been warned by Bede and Alcuin. They'd also been warned by God Herself, who sent divine signs. The *Anglo-Saxon Chronicle* reported: 'Here were dreadful forewarnings come over the land of Northumbria, and woefully terrified the people: these were amazing sheets of lightning and whirlwinds, and fiery dragons were seen flying in the sky. A great famine soon followed these signs, and shortly after in the same year, on the sixth day before the ides of January, the woeful inroads of heathen men destroyed God's church in Lindisfarne island by fierce robbery and slaughter.'

Oh, how Bede in heaven must have gloated. Meanwhile Alcuin on Earth recorded: 'Never before has such terror appeared in Britain as we have now suffered from a pagan race. The heathens poured out the blood of saints round the altar and trampled on the bodies of saints in the temple of God, like dung in the streets.'

The British poet Percy Bysshe Shelley (1792–1822) reckoned: 'History is a cyclic poem written by time upon the memories of man.'

The *real* cycle of history is that every few decades it is rewritten. The French novelist Stendhal said that the biography of Napoleon would have to be rewritten every six years. Assessments of the Vikings don't change *that* regularly, but the pendulum has swung to both extremes.

To the Victorians, the Vikings were monstrous and bloodthirsty raiders, famous for rape and pillage. In the revisionist twentieth century they were portrayed as lovable farmers and settlers who took their wives and families with them to make a peaceful living. Swords? Nah, they were ploughshares. If they *were* violent it was just because they lived in violent times . . . and those nasty Saxons were just as cruel to the poor Vikings, who probably came bearing cuddly toys. By the end of the twentieth century, the Norse were actually proto-feminists and early multiculturalists. Hillary Clinton, US politician and former First

Lady,* said that Viking society gave women considerable freedom to trade and participate in political and religious life.

It's good to change your mind, but only when you were wrong in the first place. Yes, the Vikings were city founders, brilliant seafarers and traders. But they also had a proverb: 'Put to the sword those that disagree.' (Call it the Norse code.) They founded cities with gleeful violence, they sea-fared in order to find new lands to settle and they traded in human misery — the top Norse export was slaves.

So the pendulum is swinging back. Vikings? Murderous bastards.† They stole anything they could. Churches were tourist trinket shops to be looted. The Vikings took cattle, money and food. They took the fit young victims as slaves and butchered the ones too old to fetch a good price. They had no compunction about burning down settlements and leaving a trail of destruction. Surely a peaceful settler would occupy the defeated farmer's house, not destroy it?

Let's review the worst of the crimes allegedly committed by the Scandinavians:

- Ivar the Boneless is said to have been sadistically cruel. According to the sagas, he put King Edmund of East Anglia up against a tree and had his men shoot arrows at him until his head exploded. He was turned round — some versions say

---

* Hillary was born in 1947 so she will soon be old enough to become president.
† Don't blame me for the language: it was the mild-mannered *Spectator* that said, 'They were, as we first thought, violent bastards.'

before he was dead – and his ribs were cut free of the spine, then pulled out so they looked like wings. His lungs followed through the wounds in his back. It was known as the blood eagle.

- Roger of Wendover told of the Abbess Ebba of Coldingham Monastery. This holy lady knew her community would be raided by Vikings the next day. She led her nuns in slicing off their noses and lips with a razor to make themselves too ugly to rape. Roger regrets that the Danes were so upset at having their prizes ruined that they slaughtered everyone anyway.
- In 787 (six years before the notorious Lindisfarne raid) three boatloads of Vikings landed on the Dorset coast to trade. A Saxon tax officer ordered them to appear before the king. The chronicles said: 'And in the days of King Bertric came first three ships of the Northmen from the land of robbers. The [official] then rode thereto and would drive them to the king's town; for he knew not what they were and there was he slain. These were the first ships of the Northmen that sought the land of English nation.' Murdering a tax inspector? Not all bad, then.
- The Vikings raided Britannia on holy days when they knew the towns would be full of pilgrims, women and children going to church. These unarmed people would be snatched and sold as slaves as far away as North Africa. For balance, I have to point out that the Saxons weren't a lot better. The Church objected to Christians like themselves being sold as slaves; they didn't object to other people being made slaves.
- Worse was the repeat nature of the raids. The Vikings, like burglars returning over and over again to the same houses, refused to leave their victims alone.

- Brithnoth was an old but brave Saxon warrior. The Vikings landed on the little island of Northey in the River Blackwater near Maldon, Essex. Brithnoth's army faced them from the bank of the river, across the shallow water. The island was joined to the shore by a strip of mud at low tide. As the Vikings tried to cross, Brithnoth's men cut them down. The Vikings said: 'Brithnoth. We cannot fight like this. Let my men cross to the shore and give you a real battle.' Only a numpty would say 'Yes'. Brithnoth said 'Yes'. Brithnoth was a brave and heroic man. He was soon a brave and heroic corpse. The Vikings honoured his courage as a noble enemy by cutting him into little pieces.
- In 1005 Alphege became archbishop of Canterbury. Six years later the Danes invaded southern England and captured Canterbury. They held Alphege and rich nobles for ransom. The ransoms were paid, and the others released, but the price demanded for Alphege was an astronomical three thousand gold marks. Alphege knew the poverty of his people and refused to pay or let anyone else pay for him. The Danes, at the end of a drunken feast, brought him out and asked him once again for the cash. Again, the archbishop refused so they threw large bones from the feast at him till the archbishop fell to his knees and finally an axeman delivered the coup de grâce. 'His holy blood fell on the ground and his holy soul was sent forth to God's kingdom.' Chops for the feast, the big chop for Alphege.
- Cnut, who we'll be hearing more from later, was king of England from 1016, king of Denmark from 1018 and king of Norway from 1028 until his death in 1035. Malcolm II of

Scotland also submitted to him, so Cnut could lay claim to being the first 'British' king. (Scottish acceptance of a union with England didn't last beyond the death of Cnut.) Even an allegedly 'wise' Viking king like Cnut ruled with terror. He took Saxon hostages in East Anglia. When he was attacked by the Saxons he set sail into the English Channel. Cnut dropped the hostages off in Kent – but only after he'd dropped their hands and noses off in the sea.

- There were some English leaders that Cnut didn't trust. They had promised to obey him, but he wasn't sure. Just to be on the safe side he executed them. Earl Uhtred of Northumbria, for example, went to make peace with Cnut. On Cnut's apparent order, Uhtred's own treacherous servant, Wighill, ran out from a hiding place and murdered him.

On the other side of the coin, the Saxons could be ruthless too. Geneva Convention rules did not apply for another millennium. In 2010 it was reported that fifty decapitated bodies had been found in Weymouth, thought to be executed Viking captives. It was also said that Ælla – king of Northumbria – captured the Viking leader Ragnar Lodbrok and had him put to death in a pit of snakes.* Ragnar's sons, bent upon revenge, invaded

---

* Admittedly I have questions about this. Ælla went to the trouble to dig a pit too deep for a man to climb out of; he had the countryside scoured for poisonous snakes, which are not exactly easy to find in England, then dropped Ragnar into the pit? Very entertaining, but a lot of trouble when a simple axe to the brain-box would have done the job. Not what you'd call 'credible'.

Northumbria in 866 – that's a historical fact. Norse sources claim that Ragnar's sons tortured Ælla to death with the blood eagle.

One English king led the fightback to secure his kingdom against the Danes. He was King Alfred (849–99) – later labelled Alfred the Great. He was one of the few British monarchs ever to be labelled 'Great'. But Alfred wasn't revered as a great warrior; his personal exploits against the Vikings were underwhelming. Chronicler Geoffrey of Monmouth made sure that warrior-king status went to King Arthur. Off the battlefield, Alfred was just plain dull. It took a monk called Asser to inject a little glitter into Alf's biography with a tale of burnt cakes.

One day a peasant woman, the wife of a cowherd, was making cakes, and asked a soldier sitting by the fire to keep an eye on them. The soldier was looking after his bow and arrows and perhaps a bit distracted by thoughts of Vikings and blood eagles. The poor woman saw that the cakes she'd put over the fire were burning. She ran up and took them off and scolded the soldier. 'Look there, man. Couldn't you see the cakes were burning? Why didn't you turn them over? I'm sure you'd be the first to eat them if they were nicely done.' The miserable woman did not realize that this was King Alfred, who had fought so many wars against the pagans and won so many victories.

The story is almost certainly a fiction. But it makes Alf look like a struggling soldier, driven into hiding alone to plot his comeback. What a hero he must have been to rise from that to defeat the Vikings, you'd say. Alfred is remembered for stories like this. But he could be a pragmatist too, and despite making few grand military gestures, he found ways to win.

The Chinese general Sun Tzu (545–470 BC) wrote in *The Art*

of War: 'It may be advisable not to stir forth, but rather to retreat, thus enticing the enemy in his turn; then, when part of his army has come out, we may deliver our attack with advantage.' Alfred proved adept at retreating and then re-emerging when he was better equipped to win. He then strengthened his kingdom's defences with a network of fortified sites that created 'fortress Wessex'. The Vikings were unable to penetrate them and crush the last Saxon kingdom. Alfred organized a rota of national service so he could keep forces in the field or respond to attacks quickly. He also overhauled his naval forces, bringing in experienced Frisian sailors to help with his new designs for ships. Nine hundred years later, his creation of a strong navy was what James Thomson celebrated in the song 'Rule Britannia'.

Alfred fought alongside his brother King Æthelred and they beat the Danish army at Ashdown, but the triumph at Ashdown was reversed just two weeks later at the Battle of Basing in 871. Guthrum, a Danish chieftain, became the most serious enemy for Alfred, with his army raiding Wessex. Alfred met him in a series of skirmishes, but Guthrum's hopes of crushing the Saxons came to an end with the Battle of Edington in May 878. His Danes were chased to Chippenham and besieged for ten days, until Guthrum agreed to surrender. King Alf didn't follow up by driving them out of Britannia. He made a deal whereby they kept the North East (the land of 'Danelaw') and the Saxons kept the South West.

There had been four Saxon kingdoms at the time of Alfred's birth; by his death all but Wessex had been overrun by the Vikings, and their kings killed or exiled. Alfred was the survivor. Britannia was drawing in her horns and retreating into fortress

Wessex. Denmark accepted the compromise of 'Have your cake – but we'll keep our slice.' The German politician Ludwig Erhard (1897–1977) summed up this negotiating strategy best when he said: 'Compromise is the art of dividing a cake in such a way that everyone believes he has the biggest piece.'

It is Æthelred the Unready who is renowned for coming up with the idea of paying the Vikings to go away and leave England alone.* The Vikings took their blackmail money – 'Danegeld' – and of course came back for more.

The English writer Rudyard Kipling (1865–1936) summed it up humorously but accurately in his poem 'Dane-Geld':

> It is always a temptation to an armed and agile nation
> To call upon a neighbour and to say:–
> 'We invaded you last night – we are quite prepared to fight,
> Unless you pay us cash to go away.' [. . .]
> And that is called paying the Dane-geld;
> But we've proved it again and again,
> That if once you have paid him the Dane-geld
> You never get rid of the Dane.

In 1002 Æthelred the Unready recorded in a charter that he ordered: 'A most just extermination of all the Danish men who were among the English race'. Æth wasn't thrilled to be paying

---

* 'Unready' was originally used in the sense of 'ill-advised' but has come to mean, well . . . 'not ready'. That rather shifts the blame on to the poor bloke.

Danegeld, but he decided to draw the line when he found out about a Danish plot to assassinate him. The charter also recorded how, on that day, the Danes in Oxford fled to St Frideswide's Church expecting to find refuge, but instead were pursued by the townspeople, who then set the church on fire with the Danes inside. (In 2008, archaeologists uncovered at least thirty-five skeletons at St John's College, Oxford. The bones were charred – but not the soil around them. It suggests that the story of Vikings burnt alive is true.) In other parts of the country, Viking women were said to have been buried alive. Their babies were picked up by the feet, swung round the attacker's head and smashed against a doorpost.

King Æthelred the Unready has been pilloried by historians because he paid fortunes in Saxon money for the Danish Vikings to go away, which they then declined to do. Ironically, it was a Dane who came closest to uniting Britannia for the first time.

Cnut was a Viking, but also one of the rare monarchs renowned as the Great for his powerful rule. He arrived in 1015 to pillage the lands of Edmund Ironside – Æthelred the Unready's son. As in Alfred's time, the English and the Danes battled one another to a standstill and again divided England between them. But Edmund died mysteriously, and Cnut was able to rule as the first king of a unified England. So what happened to Edmund, you ask? You don't want to know . . . oh, if you insist.

Edmund was lured to a feast. He needed the toilet (as you do). The little boys' room was the only place he went without his bodyguard. It was therefore the only place his enemy could kill him. What happened next is a mystery. Some say an agent of Cnut, a man called Edric Streona, hid in the toilet pit and stabbed the king as he sat down. According to another story there was a loaded bow and arrow in the toilet. When the king sat down the bow went off and sent an arrow up into his guts.* It seems that Edric Streona went to Cnut to claim a reward for disposing of Edmund. He must have been so very pleased when Cnut told him: 'I will raise you higher than any lord in England.' Cnut kept his promise, but not in the way Edric understood it. There are two versions: Cnut cut off Edric Streona's head and had it stuck on the top turret of his castle; or, no better for Edric, Cnut had him hanged from the tallest tree in the forest.

You may be realizing that Cnut was far from Great at times. He was a bad loser. He often cheated. When he attacked Norway in 1028 he sent large amounts of English money to princes so they would betray their king. Cnut has also become a byword for futile struggle; yet that's because the old legend has been distorted.

The original version said that Cnut was crowned at Christmas in London. He became king of all England. His nobles tried to tell him he was Lord of the Earth. Cnut had to teach them a lesson. Cnut took his throne to the edge of the Thames as the tide was coming in and told the tide to go back down. The waters rose and rose till it looked like he would drown. The toady lords begged him to come away and wise Cnut said, 'You see? There is only one Lord of the Earth and that is God.' Cnut then took off his crown and vowed never to wear it again. He hung it on a crucifix as a reminder of who was the true Lord of the Earth.

---

* The boring version is that Edmund died of wounds received in battle or from disease.

But poor Cnut's noble gesture became twisted to say that Cnut was so vain he felt he ruled the world. 'I can even rule the tide,' he boasted. One day he took his throne to the seashore as the tide was rising. 'I command you to go back,' he cried. But the tide rose over his ankles and knees. He felt a real chump so he quickly abandoned the throne and ran back to his palace. No one can stop the tide.

The truth? Probably neither version. Like the tale of Alfred and the cakes, it may have been invented to show how humble a king could be, even when he was humbly slicing off the hands and noses of hostages.

Cnut died in 1035, leaving no one to save England from any new invaders. But there was one last thrash of the Norse serpent's tail: York, 1066.

1066. The fatal year remembered by schoolchildren throughout Britain – even the ones who can't remember their school dinner money.

It started with the death of King Edward the Confessor in January 1066 and a power vacuum on the throne of England. The pretenders were a motley crew. They comprised:

- The king of Norway, Harald Hardrada aka the Thunderbolt of the North. He arrived off the north coast of England in September with a fleet of three hundred ships packed with around eleven thousand Vikings, all anxious to help him claim Cnut's throne.
- Harold Godwinson, who had been chosen as the next king of England by the king's counsellors following Edward's death.

- Harold's brother, Tostig Godwinson, who was more than willing to stab a sibling in the back in return for a fat chunk of England and allied with Hardrada.
- And, of course, Duke William of Normandy, who believed he had the right to be king of England.

A melting pot of hatred, revenge and anger. King Harold Godwinson now had a dilemma; whether to march north and confront Hardrada or to remain in the south and prepare for the invasion he was expecting from France by William. Bold Harold, a man of action, travelled from London to York, a distance of 185 miles, in just four days.

As he was journeying, the Viking armada sailed up the River Ouse near York and met in a bloody encounter with Morcar, Earl of Northumberland. Morcar held the slightly higher and drier ground and was invincible as long as he stayed there.

Hardrada's Vikings used an interesting tactic. They sent a small force to the eastern, marshy end of the ditch at the bottom of the hill but held back their main force. The Saxons saw the small Viking force and charged down the slope . . . into the marshy ground. That was the moment Hardrada chose to strike with his main force. He circled his best fighters behind Morcar's men and drove them into the deepest part of the marsh. The English were trapped in the sticky ground and slaughtered. There were so many bodies that the Vikings were able to cross the meadow by treading on corpses, like stepping-stones. Tostig and Hardrada seized York.

Hardrada did not enter the rich city. Why not? Maybe he was keen to spare his future kingdom from the effects of looting by his own men. Instead, he retired to Stamford Bridge to re-supply. He made a terrible demand of the people of York: bread, wine and 150 children as hostages. He would have his men collect them from Stamford Bridge that coming Monday, 25 September.

What a day it turned out to be. Hardrada and Tostig turned up to collect the hostages from across the county of Yorkshire. They waited for the handover at Stamford Bridge, with less than half of their army and only a minimum of weapons. Guess who turned up? Harold Godwinson.

Harold made an offer to his brother Tostig saying, 'Tostig, I offer you a third of the kingdom if you will give in.' Tostig asked what was in it for his ally, Hardrada. Harold replied, 'I offer him just seven feet . . . enough to bury him.'

Tostig decided his loyalty was to the Viking. He would fight his brother. And what a fight it was. A single Viking hero blocked the bridge and slew forty Englishmen before they could cross. The English sent a boat under the bridge, pushed a pike through the planks and stabbed him from below. Yes, echoes of Edmund being stabbed from below in the toilet. Obviously not an unusual practice. You could say bog-standard.

When the Viking shield-wall finally broke, the invading army were all but annihilated. Only twenty-four ships from the original fleet of three hundred were needed to carry the survivors back to Norway.

Harold's men swarmed over the Vikings. Hardrada, wearing little armour, took an arrow in the windpipe and died. Tostig was hacked down when he refused to surrender. He should have taken the offer of a third of the kingdom . . . a bird in the hand is worth a sword in the mush.

Harold Godwinson's English had defeated one invader. Now he headed south just in case another landed there. He left some of his exhausted northern army behind, hoping to replace them with fresh troops from the south if he needed them.

Just three days later, William the Conqueror would land his Norman invasion fleet on England's south coast. And we know how that went.

The Vikings in Ireland didn't last as long as the Vikings in England.

During his reign King Brian Boru had ordered his people to take the Vikings to their hearts and hearths, saying: 'I want you to welcome this Viking into your home as a guest. Feed him and look after him as if he was an Irish warrior.'

But by 1013 Brian had become powerful enough to attack his old mates, the Dublin Vikings. He now told his Irish people: 'Now I want you to *murder* your guest in his sleep. As soon as you have done it light a torch and show it outside your house.'

That night thousands of torches burnt outside Irish homes.

The conflict between the native Irish and the Viking invaders came to a head in the Battle of Clontarf (north of Dublin) in 1014. The Vikings weren't completely driven out of Dublin and Ireland after the battle, but they were never as strong again.

When Brian Boru arrived at Clontarf, the night before the battle, the Viking leader Brodir sailed off into the Irish Sea. It was the usual trick, of course. As soon as it grew dark Brodir sailed back to Clontarf and landed.

The battle began with single combats in the old Celtic style. They weren't conclusive. One Viking leader fought an Irish leader, but each man fell with his enemy's sword in his body and his enemy's hair clutched in his hands. If it had been a football match it would had been scored as a draw. When the armies joined in, the Irish were dominant. Viking leader Brodir was beaten and ran into the woods to hide. Many more Vikings ran for the safety of their ships. But the tide had come in and they were too tired to swim. Brian Boru's fifteen-year-old grandson Tordhelbach chased two Vikings into the ocean and dragged them under. (He also managed to drown himself, which is a bit of a stupid thing to do.)

The Vikings had lost, but it wasn't all over yet. Brodir, hiding in the woods, saw Brian Boru, unguarded as his men were pursuing the defeated enemy. Brian was on his knees, praying. At first Brodir took his enemy for a priest and walked away. But Brodir's friend, who had recognized Brian, shouted, 'King! King!' and they turned back. Brodir rushed at Brian and lopped off his head with one blow of his axe. He cried: 'Now let man tell man that Brodir killed Brian.'

Brodir was captured soon after. Brian's brother gave orders for Brodir to die a slow and painful death. Not only did six thousand of his men die, but most of the Viking leaders died too. Clontarf was one of the bloodiest battles in Irish history. The monks who chronicled it wrote that blood dripped from the trees.

The Vikings' rule in England and Ireland may have been over, but they were still a force in the north-west of Scotland for another two hundred years. In the 1240s the Norwegian Vikings ruled Iceland and Greenland as well as the Hebrides. But in 1249 Alexander II of Scotland wanted to claim back the west coast islands and invaded.

The conflict raged on for a decade, but Alexander died of a

fever as his fleet attacked. This didn't end the fighting, as Alexander III of Scotland was eager to finish the war his father had started. His raids on the Norse islands in 1262 were brutal. Haakon of Norway took personal command of a defending fleet of 120 ships and up to twenty thousand men at his command. A storm wrecked that mighty fleet and Haakon struggled ashore with just a thousand men to hold off the Scottish army at Largs. He survived a year before dying in 1263. His son made peace – so long as the Scots paid him to go away ... the old Danegeld became the Norwaygeld. The Scots let the Norwegians keep the Shetland and Orkney Islands. But in time those islands started to look to Scotland for leadership. Another area was coming under Scottish rule and would ultimately form part of a United Kingdom. And so the battle at Largs signalled the end of the Viking age in Britannia.

We don't often talk about the Vikings as a unifying force, but they united Ireland against them under Brian Boru before being expelled after Clontarf in 1014; they united England against them under Cnut the Great, until he died in 1035 and his raiders were defeated at Stamford Bridge in 1066; they united Scotland under Alexander III when they lost at the Battle of Largs in 1263.

It was always a set battle against a powerful king that ended the Viking influence. They were best when they were murdering defenceless monks. If they had stuck to that, we might now be singing 'Rule ye Vikings, Ye Vikings rule the waves'.

So where does Scandinavia stand in Britannia's list of 'less happier lands'? Not very high. The national memory says they'll pillage your village, cut off your hands and steal your cake. But as enemies they did a great job of uniting the British against them.

4

FRANCE

The land of frogs' legs (detached), can-can dancer legs (attached), disgruntled farmers, champagne, berets and Maigret. If linking France to 'frogs' sounds rather racist these days, then there is a noble precedent: Gloriana herself, Queen Elizabeth I.

In the 1570s the queen was engaged to the Frenchman Francis, Duke of Anjou. She called him her 'Frog', some say because of his energetic hopping around the dance floor. Far from taking it as an insult, the delighted Francis sent Elizabeth a frog earring, which she wore in remembrance of him.

The alliance of an English queen with a French nobleman was not universally popular. Writers William Page and John Stubbs wrote that Elizabeth was 'blindly and helplessly leading her country into slavery by the French'. The offensive hands that wrote those words were chopped off to encourage other authors to think again.* Or, Elizabeth might have said, *Pour encourager les autres*.

---

* Isn't it apt that a man whose arm ended at the wrist was called Stubbs? Not so fitting for Page, who wouldn't be writing many more of those after his indiscretion.

Elizabeth's Frog may have led to the nickname for the French, or it could have been the French habit of eating frogs' legs (like we eat *rosbif*). Or it could even have come from the French themselves; two hundred years after Elizabeth's reign, the French labelled the people of Paris *les Grenouilles*, or Frogs.

But we digress. We can see that mistrust of the French was deep-seated even in Tudor times. Where did it come from?

In 911 the (aptly named) Charles the Simple, king of France, gave land in northern France to the Viking Rollo and his people. The neighbours were nervous of the 'North-men', which soon became 'Nor-men'. Just like their Viking forebears, these Normans had a taste for travel and conquest. At first they focused their attentions to the south – Italy and Sicily. But then Normandy was inherited by one Duke William aka the Bastard (for reasons you may like to guess). William turned his attention to the island across the Channel.

William had a traumatic childhood, always in danger of being murdered by people who wanted his land. As a result, he grew up tough. He survived his first major battle in 1047, at Val-ès-Dunes, at the age of just nineteen. Historian William of Poitiers said: 'Young William was not scared at the sight of the enemy swords. He hurled himself at his enemies and terrified them with slaughter. Some of the enemy met their death on the field of battle, some were crushed and trampled in the rush to flee, and many horsemen were drowned as they tried to cross the River Orne.'

William later marched on the town of Alençon. The defenders barred its gates and then made fun of his mother's family. They dangled cow hides over a castle wall and mocked William with cries of 'Leather. Leather for the leather-worker's grandson.' This did not go down well. When William eventually captured the town, he took thirty-two of the leading citizens of Alençon and paraded them in front of the townsfolk. Then he had their hands and feet cut off. The message to the world was, 'You don't mess with William.' The people of Britain found this out the hard way.

In 1064, as we saw in the last chapter, Harold Godwinson of England was the man most likely to take the English throne after Edward the Confessor. But the Norman chroniclers record that one day, while Harold was crossing the English Channel, his ship was caught in a storm. Harold was recognized and taken to Duke William of Normandy.

William also fancied himself as king of England. The captive Harold had to promise he would let William become king when Ed the Confessor died. We can understand why Harold would make such a promise when the alternative was a life in captivity. We can also understand why he had no intention of keeping that promise. Sure enough, William set him free . . . and Harold denied he had said anything of the sort. (As another Queen Elizabeth – the Second – was known to remark, 'Recollections may vary'.)

This is the story told by Norman historians who want to show that Harold was a rotten cheat who broke his promises and noble William was the rightful king of England – not William the Conqueror, but William 'I've-just-popped-over-the-Channel-to-take-what-is-rightfully-mine-old-chap'.

Yes, that's right. It's 1066. We've reached the Battle of Hastings. Like most invasions of Britain, there is a story about the common soldiers being reluctant to engage with the Brits without receiving a plucky speech. This time it was William's minstrel, Taillefer, who was the hero of the hour – or at least for about ten minutes. The Norman soldiers looked up at Harold and his Saxons on the top of Senlac Hill and didn't fancy their chances. That's when Taillefer rode forward, as the Norman historian Wace recounts. An all-round entertainer at William's court, Taillefer performed one of his tricks – juggling his sword. Then he charged the English lines alone, 'while the troops marched behind singing the Song of Roland'. That was an epic poem about the Battle of Roncevaux Pass, in which the knight Roland died a courageous death. Perhaps not the best choice of song when you are going courageously into a sword-fight. Taillefer killed the first Saxon soldier who came at him but then he was butchered. Still, Taillefer would have been pleased to know that his example went on to shame and encourage the Normans to victory.

As well as the familiar tale of a 'Leap, fellow soldiers' figure, there was the other regular trope at the Battle of Hastings: the tactic of pretending to run away to draw the enemy away from their secure position. When the Saxons followed the Norman 'retreat' the Normans turned and butchered the Saxons. They hadn't read enough history books.

To this day, one of the great myths of British history is that King Harold fell at the Battle of Hastings when an arrow struck him in the eye. The Bayeux Tapestry does show a man falling with an eyeful of arrow near the inscription saying Harold is slain. But the documentary history doesn't back that up. Writing nearer the time, Guy of Amiens in his 'Song of the Battle of Hastings' claims:

Harold himself was slain, pierced with mortal wounds. Four knights bore arms for the destruction of the king. The first, cleaving his breast through the shield with his point, drenched the earth with a gushing torrent of blood; the second smote off his head below the protection of the helmet and the third pierced the inwards of his belly with his lance; the fourth hewed off his thigh and bore away the severed limb: the ground held the body thus destroyed.

A pretty comprehensive job, assuming we believe Guy. He had been suspended as bishop by the pope, who felt William of Normandy could do no wrong. Guy wrote his poem in praise of William in the hope of getting back into the pope's good books. (It didn't work.)

The waters are further muddied by William of Malmesbury, who relates the same incident in the *Gesta Regum Anglorum*, more than fifty years after the battle. There, he does refer to an arrow. 'This alteration of fortune, now one side prevailing and now the other, held as long as Harold lived. Harold, fell from having his brain pierced with an arrow, receiving the fatal blow from a distance, he yielded to death. The English fled without respite till the night.' One of the knights then hacked at Harold's thigh with a sword as he lay on the ground, and was stripped of his knighthood by William for a dastardly and shameful act.

Was William the Conqueror infected by some spirit of English fair play? Did he really send a knight home in disgrace for disrespecting the corpse of a noble opponent? It doesn't quite fit with William's reputation as a ruthless sadist. But, truth or fiction, the arrow in the eye story stuck – like an arrow in the eye.

The English weren't beaten by a superior Norman enemy. They were beaten by sheer bad luck. William the Conqueror may have conquered – the clue is in the name – but it's one thing winning a prize and another holding on to it.

The Saxons were all but enslaved and it seems they never forgave or forgot. The French would be the subject of English love and hate for the next 950 years. Saxon lands were given to Norman lords, who built castles and cathedrals to tower over the conquered people and keep them cowed. Today those symbols of Norman oppression and enslavement are tourist attractions. The Saxon serfs weren't attracted.

There were sporadic rebellions across Britain, but they weren't coordinated – they didn't inspire the Saxons to unite. Still, William had his work cut out for him. In 1069 the English revolted in the south while Edric the Wild went wild in the west. In Yorkshire the old English enemies, the Vikings, sailed across the North Sea to help Prince Edgar's resistance.

The Vikings marched on York. The Norman defenders set fire to the city and left the safety of York Castle to fight the enemy in open battle. They were wiped out.

North of York, in Durham, the locals murdered the Norman lord sent to rule them, Robert of Comines. William's response to these revolts was revolting. He razed the region. Houses and farms were burnt. Livestock was killed so that the Saxon natives faced starvation. Corpses were left to rot by the side of the road and some say that Saxon survivors turned to cannibalism to stay alive. The vicious assault became known as 'the Harrying of the North'. Even William himself, on his deathbed, said he regretted it.

In Durham the Normans eventually tried to gain the trust, or at least the awe, of the natives. The revered St Cuthbert had been buried in a humble church of wood as befitted a notoriously humble man. Saxon pilgrims had always gathered at his tomb as their most sacred place. The Normans pinched Cuthbert's coffin and placed it in a grotesque monstrosity called Durham Cathedral, so the conquered people had to worship in a symbol of Norman power. The message was, 'Look on my works, ye Mighty, and despair.'*

In the east there was Hereward the Wake (1035–c.1072), an Anglo-Saxon nobleman and local resistance leader. In 1071 William the Conqueror personally led an army against Hereward's base at the Isle of Ely. It was a marshy island that was surrounded by fens and William gave up. After all, he was playing the long game in trying to dominate the whole of Britain. The Normans could simply wait till Hereward died. The Saxon hero obliged a year later.

The Scots had a different take on the conquest. Not a threat so much as an opportunity. A chance to invade England. In 1070, Malcolm III had marched into England and allied himself with Edgar the Ætheling, the last Anglo-Saxon claimant to the English throne.

In 1072, William the Conqueror led an army to deal with Malcolm. The armies met at Abernethy and they signed a treaty. Malcolm agreed to acknowledge William as his overlord and to stop rooting for Edgar. Malcolm broke that treaty regularly, but in

---

*   Though it was Shelley who put it so eloquently.

1093 he was killed in a battle against the Normans, ending the first phase of Scottish resistance. Then, in 1138, David I of Scotland invaded England and captured Carlisle for a while, though it was a short-lived triumph. Maybe it did help to delay the Norman conquest, since Scotland remained independent for several centuries.

The Irish also saw the invasion of England as an opportunity. In 1166 the king of Leinster, Dermot MacMurrough, invited Henry II to come to Ireland to sort out his old enemy Rory O'Connor. Henry sent Richard, Earl of Pembroke, known as 'Strongbow'. In 1170 Strongbow's army landed in Waterford on the south-east coast. The Norman leader decided to terrorize the people into giving in. So he didn't simply execute seventy Waterford leaders – he took them to Baginbun Head, chopped off their arms, legs and heads and threw the bits into the creek. Look on Strongbow's works, ye Irish, and despair.

Strongbow married his host's daughter, so that, when Dermot MacMurrough died, Strongbow took his throne. Crafty. Naturally, Strongbow ended up taking over a large part of Ireland. The Irish believed Dermot MacMurrough's punishment was that he rotted to death for this great sin. It saw the beginning of Anglo-Norman supremacy of the island that lasted for hundreds of years until . . . Well, you'll see in Chapter 9.

The Welsh battled gamely as their Silures ancestors had done against the Romans. Some, like Rhys ap Tewdwr in Deheubarth (south-west Wales), had made a deal with William the Conqueror, but rebels threw Rhys out in 1088. He hopped across to Ireland to ask the Vikings to fight for him, promising that their payment would be all the Welsh men and women they could capture as slaves. It worked. Rhys won back his possessions in

Wales with Viking help. Some Welsh must have suffered a trip to the Dublin slave market – the largest in Europe.

Resistance eventually gave way to integration. In 1205 Llywelyn the Great married Joan, daughter of King John of England, making Llywelyn top man in Wales. Then in 1267 Henry III of England made Llywelyn the Great's grandson, Llywelyn ap Gruffudd, the 'Prince of Wales', mainly to stop him attacking England. Bit by bit, the warring tribes of these islands were merging to create a single, dominant leader, through intermarriage and alliances. And kidnapping.

In 1272 Edward I became king and set about turning England into 'Britain'. His plan for Wales was simple: batter them into submission. In two campaigns (1277 and 1282) Edward fought brutal wars to crush Welsh princes like Llywelyn ap Gruffudd. The princes were killed, and thus ended Welsh dreams of independence.

Edward was devious enough to employ ruthless tactics like having Llywelyn's bride Eleanor kidnapped on the way to her wedding. In 1282 Llywelyn got into a scrap and died. He is remembered as 'Llywelyn the Last Leader'. England now ruled Wales and Ed built massive castles to make sure it stayed that way. The Statute of Rhuddlan (1284) incorporated Wales into England, where English laws replaced Welsh customs. Edward established new towns for English settlers to replace Welsh communities. There were further Welsh rebellions down the years, but they were against 'English' domination, not French. And a vision of a united Wales has never gone away. Edward I only gave the Welsh a common enemy.

The first British king to speak English as his first language is usually accepted as being Henry IV (1367–1413), who ruled from 1399 to 1413. The French conquerors had been conquered by the forces of assimilation, and it helped to make England a more unified and cohesive country. If there was to be a unified Britannia then it would be unified under overlords from England ... and the Scots, Welsh and Irish weren't having that.

Now that the Norman French had been absorbed into England, they could strike up an enmity with France. There had been an inherent weakness in William's conquest: the good old English Channel. The Norman kings and their nobles had their 'old' lands in France and their 'new' lands in Britain. They were headed down a river with a foot in two canoes. Sooner or later, they were going to have to choose ... France, Britain, or drown. The English Saxons gave very little trouble. The Welsh, Scots and Irish, on the fringes of Norman power, stirred things up, but it was on the French side of the Channel that trouble eventually spilt over into a long war between the nations.

For three hundred years England's Norman kings spoke French, thought in French and probably dreamt in French. When their subjects in France rebelled, or were attacked, then the English lords paddled across to defend them. In 1337, King Philip VI of France confiscated the English duchy of Aquitaine from King Edward III of England. Three years later, Edward III retaliated by claiming the French throne. (His mum had been Isabella of France.) They fought for 116 years – so it became known as the Hundred Years' War. Which proves there are just three types of mathematician: those who can add up and those who can't.

England and France fought through the Black Death ... and

rampaging soldiers helped to spread it, of course. They fought through Peasants' Revolts (on both sides of the moat). They fought their Celtic neighbours, and they fought one another in the bits between. (Well, it kept them in practice.) Britannia loves the brave little hero winning through. The legends of the Hundred Years' War are the legends of the plucky English with their pluckier little Welsh archers, beating the massed hordes of Burgundy and any other wine you care to name.

Phase one of the Hundred-and-sixteen Years' War – from 1337 to 1360 – could be called the Edwardian Wars. It started when Edward III of England hammered the Scots and set off to do the same to the French. After all, his Uncle Charles had been king of France so why shouldn't Ed follow in his armour-plated steps? Philip VI of France begged to differ and told Ed to *allez* off.

The first major fisticuffs was at Crécy, northern France, in 1346. The statistics show that the English David was ranged against the monstrous French Goliath: Edward's army of eighteen thousand had less than four thousand armoured knights. He faced Philip's thirty-eight thousand men including twelve thousand knights. How could they win?

The English waited on a small hill. The French had to cross a stream and attack uphill (but this was not necessarily a problem for the knights, just their horses). As the two armies faced one another there was a shower of rain. The English took the strings off their longbows to keep them dry. The French archers used crossbows, which were much harder to unstring quickly, and the downpour made them pretty useless. The sun then came out, straight in the eyes of the French. Although they couldn't make out the enemy forces very clearly, they could see that the English archers were at the front. Behind the archers the English knights were waiting on foot. It looked as though the English knights wouldn't reach their horses in time if there was a melee.

Philip's tactics seemed sound: first send the crossbowmen forward. Shoot holes in the rows of English archers. Then send the knights on horseback through the gaps and cut down the English knights on foot. Regardless of the specific tactics, his force was so huge it should have defeated the English no matter what. So what happened next? The few crossbowmen with dry strings fired and were met by deadly showers of arrows from the English longbows. They stumbled back and were trampled by their own knights moving forward. The powerful longbows punched holes in the French armour too. Philip the foolish hadn't seen that one coming.

Horses and knights fell, more horses and knights stumbled over them. When a few knights did get through they were surrounded and pulled down by the English knights on foot. Ten thousand French fighters died and King Philip was wounded by an arrow in the neck but escaped with his life. His victory secured, the English King Edward could now claim to be king of France.

In the first international clash of the European championship, the score is England 1 – 0 France.

The game was postponed for a while, since both teams had quite a few players sidelined with injuries due to the Black Death. The next of the big battles in the Hundred-and-sixteen Years' War was at Poitiers in 1356. The English army was small, but the French made big mistakes. They should have attacked on Sunday, when the English were tired after their march and were still building their defences of stakes and ditches. A surprise French attack would have had a high chance of success. But the French king, John II, known as 'the Good', was pious and told them it was sinful to fight on a Sunday. Then, on the Monday of the battle, the French knights remembered Crécy and fought on foot as the English had back then, not horseback. A big mistake.

The little English army fought desperately for seven hours and finally surrounded King John. His knights fought and died to save him. The French historian Froissart described the battle as very, very bloody:

> Some of the French knights are cut in the belly and tread on their own guts. Others vomit their teeth. Some, still standing, have their arms cut off. The dying roll about in the blood of strangers, the fallen bodies groan. The ghosts, flying from the lifeless bodies, moan horribly. The bodies pile up around the waving battle-axe of King John. His helmet is knocked off and he bleeds from wounds in the face. 'Surrender,' an English voice cries. 'Surrender or you are a dead man.' A French rebel is the first of the English army to reach the king. 'Give yourself up and I will lead you safely to the English prince.' King John hands him his glove as a sign of surrender.

King John was taken as a hostage to England until a vast ransom was paid. France was left without a king and many parts were 'ruled' by gangs of robbers for almost ten years.

England 2 – France 0, and it's not even half time.

On Monday, 13 April 1360, the powerful English army was shattered by an enemy more powerful than the French. Edward III's army was camped near Chartres when a hailstorm hit them. The storm killed men, killed horses, turned tents to shreds of fabric and dragged and crushed the supply wagons into the mud. Many who survived the storm, lacking shelter, died of the cold. Shattered King Edward made peace with the French.

England 2 – 1 France.

The comeback was on, so why didn't France counter-attack and invade England? After all, William the Conqueror hadn't waited for the English to come and put the boot into France. So why, in 116 years of war, didn't his French successors cross the English Channel and invade, you ask.

And I answer, they did. Or they tried. In 1386 England had sent an army off to fight in Spain. The Scots promised to invade from the north of England if France crossed the Channel to invade from the south. The French were bosom buddies with the Scots. The French claimed their fleet was to be 'the greatest since God created the world'. God may have pointed out that Noah's fleet of one ark hadn't done such a bad job in saving all sentient life. But God remained silent, as She so often does.

The French bought and built twelve hundred ships, which sounds impressive, but in reality some were a bit worm-eaten in the hulls and moth-eaten in the sails. They engineered a flat-pack 'camp' that was to be towed across the Channel and assembled into a fortress when they landed – an idea borrowed from Julius Caesar and William the Conqueror. The fortress would be nine thousand paces round the walls. Those walls would be six metres high, with towers every twenty metres. They also had two hundred thousand arrows (about ten to kill each English defender). However, they may have been too drunk to fire straight because they had brought four million litres of wine with them – enough for fifty litres per fighter.

The huge French fleet amassed in an area of northern European coast known as the Scheldt to wait for the mighty Duke of Berry to arrive for their great sea battle. The Duke of Berry was otherwise engaged. He liked collecting things – books and paintings and musical instruments and the usual stuff. He also collected dogs and religious 'relics' – bits of holy people and holy things. He had enough of the Virgin Mary's hair to stuff a mattress. He also had a giant's tooth.

Berry finally arrived at the port on 14 October, the auspicious date when William the Conqueror won the Battle of Hastings. But the days were turning wild and wintry. Storms battered the ships – sailors lost their bottle. (With all that wine, they must have lost more than one bottle.) The French king, Berry's brother, gave up and went home, leaving the floating fortress to the Duke of Burgundy. The English didn't have four million litres of wine, but they had a pretty good party and a good laugh at the French fighting flops.

Seemingly, all England had to do now was wait. France's King Charles VI had gone mad, leaving the feeble Prince Charles in charge. The French prince conceded that Henry V and the English could have France when his dad died.

King Charles VI had suffered a psychotic episode during the Battle of Roosebeke back in 1382 against Flemish rebels. He charged into his own battle lines and killed several of his men before being restrained. He was captured and ransomed back to the French. It's not certain if either side wanted him. In 1392 his hair fell out, his nails fell off, and he grew ever more paranoid. Then in 1400, during a masque, some of Charles's men caught fire. A spark from a flaming torch set several flammable costumes on fire, including the one Charles was wearing. Believing that they were being attacked, Charles killed several of his companions. He never fully recovered from his injuries. In fact, Charles began to imagine he was made of glass, and had steel rods put into his clothes so he wouldn't shatter if he fell over.

The French were at their weakest and it was an opportunity for England to take over the French state, just as Edward had wanted to do sixty years before. It never happened, but the English idea that its monarchs were entitled to rule the French would cost many thousands of lives.

In 1415 the new king, Henry V, stirred up the Hundred Years' War again. He certainly didn't poetically say: 'Once more unto the breach, dear friends, once more; Or close the wall up with our English dead.' That was just a flourish by William Shakespeare. Yet with that speech Will Shakespeare nailed another iconic sentence to the mast of British nationalism.

Agincourt was, again, an underdog battle of a gallant Brit army against the odds. The invading Brits, under Henry V, were weakened by disease and heading back to Calais and safety when a French force blocked their way. This was it: Butch Cassidy and the Sundance Kid fighting their way out of the pass.

What had the French learnt in the sixty years since Poitiers? Not a lot. The French knights fought on foot, again. At least now their armour was heavier to keep out English arrows, but that also meant they could hardly move. The French knights pushed to the front to grab the glory, again. Their crossbows (at the back) were useless, again. The knights were so packed together they could hardly swing a cat – or a sword. Stuck in their heavy, immobile armour, the French knights slipped in the mud. The next line of knights moved forward and fell over the front line, again. The English foot soldiers saw this and dashed in to slide their knives into joints in the armour. The English were on the rampage, again.

Battles like Agincourt and Poitiers were mythologized as stories of gallant little English and Welsh forces against the massed ranks of the cream of the French military machine. But Shakespeare was writing to flatter the monarchs who paid his wages. In *Henry V*, the Bard was economical with the historical facts about Agincourt. The numbers? A chronicler from Burgundy numbered the French army as fifty thousand. Not realistic for medieval times. Modern estimates say around twelve thousand French to eight thousand English and Welsh.

Another false 'fact' is that the 'V' sign as an obscene gesture originated at Agincourt. Myth says that the French threatened to cut off the fingers of any captured English archers to stop them firing their bows. The peasant archers held up those two fingers up in a defiant 'V' sign. 'Look, lads, we still have our fingers. Up yours.' Inconveniently, there are no records of anyone removing the digits of prisoners. (Why would they? Easier just to kill them.)

Then there's the legend that the victory belonged to the Welsh archers. Their longbows, renowned for their accuracy and power, were apparently a major factor in devastating the French cavalry. Four hundred and sixty Welsh soldiers are recorded as leaving Wales, and some of those must have been the victims of the disease that swept the British camp. If (say) four hundred actually fought at Agincourt, they made up about 5 per cent of Henry V's eight thousand-strong force. They might have been useful, but probably not decisive.

Then the story persists that there was a massacre of French prisoners at the end. The French prisoners alone outnumbered Henry's army. It was said that only those worth the most in ransom were spared and the commoners were killed; but examination of the ransom contracts shows they were for all ranks, not just the super-rich. Some prisoners were killed, but not hundreds.

The Agincourt myth fuels the nationalist belief that the British (and the English in particular) are gallant little underdogs, fighting for a 'good' and 'just' cause. Henry had a legitimate claim to the throne, and he was already on the retreat, and the French army outnumbered his, and he *still* won. God must be on the side of the English.

Agincourt looked like the end for France. But Britannia had reckoned without a simple village girl named Joan.

In 1428, the nineteen-year-old Joan of Arc was looking after her sheep in a field when angels appeared. They told her to lead an army against the English. In just three years she commanded an army that beat the socks off the English and made sure Prince Charles was crowned King Charles VII of France.

In the end she was captured by the army of Burgundy and 'sold' to her English enemies. The English didn't like the idea that God was on the French side. They had to 'prove' Joan was actually working for the devil instead. They put her on trial, with 'French priests' to judge her, and – surprise! – they found her guilty. She was a witch, they said, so she was burnt.

The British are painted as villains in French history and Joan was made a saint in 1920. A blot on the copybook of Anglo–French relations. Is that fair? What, for example, did King Charles VII of France do to save the girl who had given him his crown and France its freedom? Nothing. No ransom, no rescue, no bargaining with the English. He let them burn her.

Joan's fight wasn't the end of the Hundred Years' War, but the English were never the same again. Their enemy was now fighting for a new idea – the idea that they weren't just citizens of Paris, or Normans of Normandy... they were French. The English had a fighting chance against the people of Paris and Aquitaine, Brittany and Normandy, while those regions squabbled. The English had far less chance when those regions joined together under Charles VII and called themselves France. That's why Joan, even scorched to ashes, is so important in French history. The French wars didn't unite Britannia. But they did unite France.

Over three hundred years later the French returned the compliment and waged a war so bitter it left its mark on Britain's railway stations, statues and street names to this day.

Every society, in every age, likes to copy good ideas when it sees them. The Americans looked at British taxes and held a revolution that set them free of their king in 1783. The French peasants heard about it and decided to have a go themselves. The French Revolution started just six years later.

Liberté, égalité, fraternité, they cried. With the help of the

guillotine they overthrew the posh and declared people power.*
Some Brits crossed the Channel and became lyrical about the
'*liberté*' the French were enjoying. The English poet William
Wordsworth (1770–1850) rather short-sightedly claimed the
freedom was glorious:

> Bliss was it in that dawn to be alive,
> But to be young was very Heaven. O times,
> In which the meagre, stale, forbidding ways
> Of custom, law, and statute, took at once
> The attraction of a country in romance.

Wordsworth's political brain cell was as lonely as a cloud and he should have stuck to writing about daffodils. Fifty years later, the writer Charles Dickens was – with the wisdom of hindsight – more balanced. The first paragraph of his French Revolutionary novel *A Tale of Two Cities* has been voted the best opening of any book in the English language: 'It was the best of times, it was the worst of times, it was the age of wisdom, it was the age of foolishness, it was the epoch of belief, it was the epoch of incredulity, it was the season of light, it was the season of darkness, it was the spring of hope, it was the winter of despair.'

So, Charlie, was it a good thing or a bad? Oh, it was both?

---

* After a couple of years there wasn't a lot of *liberté* because – as usual – one person rose to the top amid the chaos and imposed order on the freedom fighters by force. It's often the way revolutions end. It was Napoleon Bonaparte in the French Revolution; Vladimir Lenin in the Russian Revolution; and Adolf Hitler in the Weimar Republic.

At the time, Britain panicked. The moat of the English Channel could keep out invaders, but it couldn't keep out revolutionary ideas. Britain went to war with France in 1793 and Will Wordsworth's best mate, Samuel Taylor Coleridge (1772–1834), raged against Britannia. Britain should support the French,

> For ne'er, O Liberty! with partial aim
> I dimmed thy light or damped the holy flame;
> But blessed the paeans of delivered France,
> And hung my head and wept at Britain's name.

The British establishment demurred. The French revolutionary leader Maximilien Robespierre introduced The Terror in which 1,785 people went to the guillotine in just six weeks. That's about one every twenty minutes. It's surprising there was anyone left in Paris at that rate. In the end the French decided to chop and change, and the guillotine got Robespierre. Britons like Wordsworth changed their tune too. By 1794 he was saying, 'I recoil from the bare idea of a revolution.' By 1811 he was likening Napoleon to Milton's Satan. He discovered what all good poets know – in death there is true *egalité*.

As for *fraternité*, there wasn't a lot for the Britons to admire and copy, but credit where it's due, they were very good at liberating heads.

Joseph-Ignace Guillotin told the French Assembly in 1789: 'My machine will take off a head in a twinkling and the victim will feel nothing but a refreshing coolness. We cannot make too much haste, gentlemen, to allow the nation to enjoy this advantage.'

What Dr Guillotin didn't expect was that the death machine would be named after him. The French might have called it 'the National Razor', 'the Patriotic Shortener', 'the Goncourt Prize for Murderers' and (sweetest of all) 'the Silence Mill'. But the world still knows it as the guillotine. The Guillotin family, on the other hand, decided to change their name.

The Scots had had a mechanical axe called the Maiden. Ironically, the man who introduced it, James Douglas, was executed by his Maiden in 1581. And Halifax in Yorkshire had a mechanized chopper, 'the Halifax Gibbet', as early as 1286. So the French copied the British in capital punishment.

The good Doctor Guillotin didn't want anyone to be hurt with this machine. Who wouldn't want to feel a refreshing coolness on the neck? So he had it thoroughly tested before sending a criminal to his death. With what did he test it? A turnip? A sheep from the abattoir? No. Corpses from the local mortuary. You have to wonder what gentle humanist could pick up a corpse, lop off its head with a guillotine, gather up the bits and carry them off to bury them. Probably not William 'Bliss-was-it-in-that-dawn-to-be-alive' Wordsworth.

The French are ambivalent about their guillotine. In 2018 a guillotine was put up for auction. The Russian seller claimed it had been used during the Revolution to execute royalists ... experts said it hadn't; it was a replica. The government objected, but the sale went ahead. It was sold to French businessman Christophe Ferrier, who said: 'This is the history of France. I have been trying to buy that guillotine for years.' He added, ominously, 'I am waiting for the next revolution.'

He may be a bit short of aristocrats and royals to use it on. Never mind, Britain still has plenty they could lend.

What did the rulers of France do whenever the peasants grew restless? Sent in the army, every time.

Revolutions usually end up with the chancers taking their chance. In 1795 the French Army was winning battles but there were no great leaders. So it was time for the government to turn to a bright young (twenty-six-year-old) general, Napoleon Bonaparte. He had been hanging around Paris, whingeing about how unfairly the government was treating him. He was a shabby, long-haired little figure,* wandering the streets and threatening to kill himself when government minister Barras sent for him and said: 'Will you lead the government forces? You have just three minutes to decide.'

Big decision. Boney said 'Yes'.

The royalist rebels outnumbered the government forces. Boney had a tough job on his hands. He lined up his men and waited for the rebel attack.

He then did something the rebels didn't really expect – something which would make him a great leader. He fought dirty.

He lined up his men to confront the rebels. As they marched towards him firing muskets he ordered his men to fire back using cannon loaded with grapeshot – slugs of metal packed into a

---

* Boney was not a tall bloke, but today's psychologists say there is no such thing as 'small-man syndrome' whereby vertically challenged people compensate for their low height with high aggression.

canister like the world's biggest shotgun. Some of the shot was wired together so it would slice off limbs quite neatly. The bombardment was long and merciless. The royalists were blown away.

The British enjoy understatement and it was the Scottish historian Thomas Carlyle (1795–1881) who described Napoleon's massacre of the protestors as 'a whiff of grapeshot'.

By 6 p.m. the rebellion – and probably the French Revolution – was over. Napoleon wanted to be leader of the greatest power in Europe, and he saw Britain as his main rival. War with the old enemy was inevitable, but this time Napoleon's France was up against a united country: not just England, but Britain, which sat like a fortress behind its English Channel moat. Britannia almost ruled the waves. Almost.

The last ground invasion of Britain is almost forgotten today – it's forgotten because it failed, but we should remember it because we really were plucky underdogs this time: Britain fought off the invading army with empty cannon and pitchforks.

Napoleon knew that his best hope of success was to find a sneaky way to attack that did not involve crossing the English Channel, so he first attempted an invasion with a force of fourteen hundred soldiers landing on the west coast of Wales in 1797. He might have expected the Welsh, long oppressed by the English, to rise up and join him as he headed inland. His fourteen hundred were in for a surprise.

The troops – known as 'La Légion Noire', the Black Legion – landed at Carreg Wastad, near Fishguard, while the main French army was planning to invade Ireland and set it free from British rule. The French had actually sent the Black Legion to attack

Bristol – to make the English think *that's* where the invasion would land. But gales blew them past Bristol so they sailed round to Fishguard.

The Fishguard defenders only had eight cannon in the whole town – and those cannon only had three cannonballs. So what did the defenders do? They fired blanks. It kept the French quiet for hours as they waited for Lord Cawdor to arrive with a proper army.

The French found some barrels of wine that had been washed ashore the week before and they drank it all. There's a story that one Frenchman fell asleep in a farmhouse. He was so drunk he woke in the night and heard the click of a musket and fired at his enemy. It turned out to be the tick of a grandfather clock.

The local rich folk grabbed their money and ran away. But the peasants grabbed pitchforks and scythes and even spades and joined a Dad's Army defence force. Or a Mum's Army.

Jemima Nicholas – a local cobbler – went out into the fields that day and saw a dozen French soldiers wandering around. They were poor soldiers: half of the French army were criminals fresh out of jail. Some of them still had ankle irons on. They were starving and drunk. Jemima caught them chasing her sheep and chickens for food. Jemima picked up a pitchfork and waved it at them. They threw down their weapons. Jemima marched them down to the local lock-up.

She and her friends joined Lord Cawdor's army to capture the rest of the French on the beach – just for sport really. They caught one or two French on the way to the shore. One was bashed over the head with a chair leg, another was thrown down a well. The French on the beach saw the women's red cloaks in the distance.

They thought they were more redcoat soldiers coming to attack. They threw down their weapons. Napoleon would have been proud of them.

Jemima became a Welsh heroine, though in truth she should be revered by the rest of us too – the real Britannia. For her exploits she was awarded a pension of £50 a year for life. That's how a Welsh woman helped to stop the last invasion of Britain.*

After this defeat the French never tried invading Britain again. In fact no enemy has landed on Britain's shores since. (Unless you count a few German pilots shot down in the Second World War.)

Small-man syndrome? Horatio Nelson (1758–1805) was five feet four inches (in old money), and that was three inches shorter than Napoleon. Nelson's family tree was a bonsai.

Repelled by the Welsh cobbler and her friends, Napoleon wanted to hit Britain where it hurt – in the wallet. So he decided to invade India, from where a lot of Britain's wealth derived. There was no Suez Canal in 1798, so he set off to march through Egypt and get there the quick way. The British Navy, under Nelson, pursued them and found the French at anchor in Aboukir Bay. Nelson planned his attack . . . then had dinner with the captains of his ships, declaring heroically: 'Before this time tomorrow I shall have gained a peerage or Westminster Abbey.' (Or at least a five-foot-four-inch grave therein.)

---

* But the French army was led by an old American, Colonel William Tate. So technically the last invasion of Britain was *American*-led. Not a lot of people know that.

The French chained their ships together so the British couldn't break through. The linked line faced north. The seashore made it look too shallow for the Brits to sail round the south side of the bay ... except Nelson decided that's just what they could do. Nelson's fleet darted round the south side when the French guns were all pointing north. It was a spectacular victory.

The greatest blow was when the huge French warship *L'Orient* caught fire and its gunpowder supplies exploded. More than a thousand men were killed, including Captain Casabianca and his son, Giocante. The Brits, being Brits, honoured their enemy every bit as much as their own heroes. It was young Giocante Casabianca who went down in a timeless verse. Mrs Felicia Dorothea Hemans (1793–1835) was an Anglo-Irish poet who wrote the poem 'Casabianca':

> The boy stood on the burning deck
> Whence all but he had fled;
> The flame that lit the battle's wreck
> Shone round him o'er the dead.
>
> Yet beautiful and bright he stood,
> As born to rule the storm;
> A creature of heroic blood,
> A proud, though child-like form.

And the Brits being Brits, down the years made fun of that heroic and romantic tale, like the anonymous author of the couplet:

The boy stood on the burning deck, the flames 'round him
   did roar;
He found a bar of Ivory Soap and washed himself ashore.

Nelson defeated the French again at the Battle of Trafalgar in 1805 and now Britannia really did rule the waves.

Of course, Nelson died there, shot down by a French marksman. His body was placed in a cask of brandy and HMS *Victory*, his flagship, was towed to Gibraltar. On arrival the body was transferred to a lead-lined coffin filled with spirits of wine. The sad news was carried to England aboard (what else?) HMS *Pickle*.

Nelson's heroism did seem to unite England, as his statue was raised on a column and the square named after his last battle, Trafalgar. In the end, his body wasn't buried in Westminster Abbey but in St Paul's Cathedral.

Not all Brits approved of the dedications to Nelson. A statue called Nelson's Pillar was erected in Dublin in 1809 to commemorate the victory at Trafalgar. Nelson's Pillar was a controversial landmark. Many Irish people saw it as a symbol of British oppression and rule. In 1966 the pillar was destroyed by a bomb laid by the Irish Republican Army (IRA). The IRA claimed that the bombing was an act of defiance against British rule. The remains of Nelson's Pillar were removed and now there is nothing to mark the spot where it once stood.

In 1812 Napoleon turned against Russia. At the Battle of Borodino he had a bad bladder which made riding painful. Still, he looked at the field of corpses, Russian and French, and said: 'It is the most beautiful battlefield I have ever seen.' Beauty truly is in the eyes of the beholder.

He won that battle, but the Russian winter was freezing his French Army and they had to go home. Three hundred and eighty thousand French would die of cold and hunger and disease. By 1813 Napoleon's bad gut (colic and a peptic ulcer) made him almost too ill to command at Dresden. Then the French fought a combined army of Russians, Prussians, Swedes and Austrians and lost at Leipzig. Napoleon's illness made him drowsy, so he couldn't organize a retreat. The French Army was smashed. Sixty thousand French lost.

By 1814 Napoleon had given up and was packed off to be interned on the island of Elba. King Louis XVIII (brother of the last French king, the guillotined Louis XVI) took the throne.

But in 1815 Napoleon escaped and came back to France for one last try. This time he met the Brits at Waterloo, south of Brussels. Napoleon was suffering from piles and could hardly bear to sit on his horse. The French lost to the Brits again, this time led by the Duke of Wellington, who put the boot into the enemy. Napoleon captured, end of war.

Yet again, the French had united the Brits in support of a national hero – the Duke of Wellington, whose name is honoured on many pub signs. And of course, his greatest battle, Waterloo, whose name graces a London train station and a pop song by the Swedish pop group ABBA.

Nothing brings peace with an old enemy like a confrontation with a new enemy.

One man changed the jigsaw map of Europe. Chancellor Otto

von Bismarck united the little states into the German Empire in 1871. A new kid on the block, Germany joined the other powers in Europe in their empire-building in Africa and the Pacific. A new kid with ambitions. France just didn't see the danger. On the scale of one to ten, the threat level was about a three . . . isn't it always when a war starts?

When the Spanish throne fell vacant, the emerging German State tried to crowbar the German Prince Leopold into it. France objected. In fact, France declared war in 1870 (the Franco–Prussian War) and lost. Decades later, when the German State declared war in 1914 and invaded Luxembourg and Belgium, Britain was no longer an enemy but France's greatest ally.

It was the same in 1940 when Germany invaded France, just as they had in the First World War. This time they reached Paris and the government surrendered. Germany occupied the north of France while the French governed the south from Vichy, with an officially neutral and independent state under Marshal Philippe Pétain. As if two governments weren't a bit greedy, the French had a third: the French who escaped before the German Army arrived set up Free France, a government-in-exile in London under General de Gaulle (1890–1970). If he was grateful, he didn't show it.

After the Second World War, European countries decided that the best way to prevent more hostilities – trade wars or war-wars – was to have a common market. They decided to call it the Common Market for some reason. By then Charles de Gaulle was the French leader. He could be a little autocratic – less polite people might call him a dictator. His attitude may be summed up in his statement: 'I have heard your views. They do not harmonize with mine. The decision is taken unanimously.'

Six European countries signed up to an agreement in Rome in 1957. Britain – always seeing itself as different – declined to join. When the European Community became a great success, Britain changed its mind and applied to join in. Thankfully, it was owed a favour. Charles de Gaulle had been given asylum for his Free French government during the Second World War and Britain had been part of the D-Day invasion that had finally set France free. So, naturally, President de Gaulle would welcome his old *amis* into the European Community with open arms, wouldn't he?

De Gaulle said *'Non'*. (Not even *'Non, merci'*.) Britain asked again. De Gaulle said *'Non'* again. Yes, he vetoed Britain's membership twice. But no one lives forever, and de Gaulle died. Britain finally got to join the European Community in 1973. After centuries of war, the French had become not only allies, but part of the same political union.

Of course, having joined, there were naturally many British people who wanted to leave. Nigel Farage said: 'I love Europe. France is wonderful. It should be. We've subsidised it for forty years.' In 2016 the critics finally succeeded in a vote to leave the European Union, 52 per cent to 48 per cent. We can assume de Gaulle was looking down in delight.* As he once put it (while he was still alive): 'Patriotism is when love of your own people comes first; nationalism, when hate for people other than your own comes first.'

---

* One is assuming Monsieur de Gaulle went to heaven. If they had tried to send him to hell he'd have said *'Non'*.

5
SPAIN

Spain: the land of sun, sand, Christopher Columbus and murdering bulls.* It tortured heretics in its Spanish Inquisition and made fortunes in gold by invading swathes of South America. It is also remembered for one of the seminal events in British History – the Armada.

Britannia owed a massive debt to Spain and Columbus. He founded the transatlantic slave trade from which Queen Elizabeth I cashed in. That in turn led to the growth of the British slave trade that brought untold wealth to Britain and her empire and made fortunes for traders in places like Bristol and Liverpool. In 1792 London had twenty-two slaving ships, Bristol had forty-two and Liverpool had 131. Some estimates say that around 50 per cent of the slaves following Columbus's route across the Atlantic would die in transit.

Today's Britons abhor slavery, but contempt for the slavery business goes back a long way. In the 1790s a famous actor visited the Theatre Royal, Williamson Square, Liverpool. He was a little drunk and the audience began to boo him on stage. He stopped

---

* Yes, yes, I *know* Chris Columbus was Italian, but he was a paid employee of the Spanish monarchs and did their dirty work for them.

acting and shouted at them: 'I have not come here to be insulted by a set of wretches, every brick in whose infernal town is cemented with an African's blood.' He may have been drunk . . . but he wasn't wrong.*

Chris Columbus is known as an explorer, but he was not a seeker after knowledge. He and his Spanish paymasters were after one thing – wealth. Chris and his Spanish masters wanted gold, land, gold, slaves and gold. That's what they got. The land and the gold belonged to the indigenous people, of course, but that didn't matter to the invaders from Europe. Chris's diary entry of 13 October 1492 showed his true motives: 'At daybreak great multitudes of native men came to the shore. I listened very carefully to them and tried to find out if they had any gold. I gathered from their signs that if I sailed south I would find a king with great cups full of gold. I could conquer all of these people with just fifty men and rule them as I please.'

Before Chris returned to Spain he kidnapped maybe twenty locals. The terrible conditions on the ships meant only about seven arrived in Spain alive. They were enough to show the Spanish that these strong natives would make great slaves. Given the all-clear,

---

* If you are British, you should know that in 2006 your prime minister, Tony Blair, half-apologized on your behalf. He said, 'It is hard to believe what would now be a crime against humanity was legal at the time . . . a chance to say how profoundly shameful the slave trade was – how we condemn its existence utterly . . . express our deep sorrow that it could ever have happened.' As African leaders have pointed out, that's not exactly an apology. Saying, 'I regret the loss of your family' is not the same as saying, 'Sorry we murdered them in their beds.'

Chris headed back to America – and this time he had over twelve hundred soldiers armed with guns, swords, cannon and attack dogs.

In 1495, the Spanish rounded up five hundred indigenous Arawak people on Haiti to be sent back to Spain and took another five hundred to work for them on the islands. Half the slaves died on the journey, but Chris shrugged and said: 'Although they die now they will not always die. We can send all the slaves from here that you can sell.' But he was wrong. Forced work and dreadful diseases killed off all the Arawak in time.

Chris set a fashion for turning American natives into slaves. They were packed into ships like sardines in supermarket tins. They were locked in to stop them escaping and huge numbers died in the filthy, scorching air. The contemporary historian of Spain Peter Martyr said that you didn't need a compass to find your way along the slave ship routes: 'All you had to do was follow the trail of dead Indians that had to be thrown overboard.'

When the Spaniards ran out of American slaves, they started capturing people in Africa and taking them across the Atlantic to work there. Chris C began the terrible West African slave trade that lasted another four hundred years. No sympathy for the Spanish conquistadors, then. But once an avaricious Tudor monarch spotted a business opportunity in slavery, it would be Britannia that led the way in the trade of humans as property.

But, first, there was an easier way to fill Britannia's bottomless treasure chests. Seaway robbery. Enter Francis Drake (1542–96).

Henry VIII is remembered for his appetites for food. His younger daughter Elizabeth was more hungry for money. She rarely had any because she accumulated three thousand gowns embroidered with precious stones and 628 pieces of jewellery. All this while the people who fought to defend Britannia were left to starve in the streets.

The Spanish Flota de Indias (West Indies Fleet – also called the Silver Fleet) was a convoy system used by the Spanish Empire from 1566. Gloriana looked greedily at the Spanish treasure ships and decided she wanted a cut. The one who did the dirty work was Francis Drake. But Drake began his career with Spain's other gift to Britannia – slavery.

Drake's first major expeditions came in the 1560s, when he joined his cousin John Hawkins on some of Britain's earliest slave-trading voyages to West Africa. The pair usually secured their cargo of human misery neither by landing and capturing natives nor buying them from African traders. They cut out the middlemen by attacking Portuguese slave ships. They would then transport the slaves to the Spanish Caribbean and sell them off to local plantations. This was illegal under Spanish law, but like that other infamous sailor, Nelson, they chose to turn a blind eye.

Elizabeth allowed Francis to circumnavigate the world between 1577 and 1580. But that was a cover for a piratical expedition. Drake told Elizabeth that he would raid Spanish shipping, but it would need a lot of setting up. Someone had to pay for Drake's ships, for the supplies and a crew. If the adventure went well you'd get a share of the treasure. But it was a risk. If storms or Spanish galleons sank Drake's ships, then you'd lose all of your money.

When Drake entered the Pacific he spent several months

plundering unsuspecting galleons and sacking ports along the coast of Chile and Peru. He might have had Elizabeth's approval, but he acted like a pirate. When Drake's men captured one Spanish ship, most of the crew jumped overboard and swam ashore to escape him, but Drake captured one young sailor alive. There was no treasure on the ship, so Drake reasoned it must be somewhere on shore. Not wanting to waste time looking for it, Drake ordered a rope to be tied over one of the ship's spars. He tied the sailor's hands and stood him on the edge of the ship. Then he placed the rope round his neck. Drake put a hand against the young man's knee and pushed him till he tumbled off the side.

The sailor screamed as he fell, and the scream stopped when the sailor hit the water. The rope round his neck had not been fastened and it didn't choke the prisoner. When he resurfaced, Drake told him to hold on to the rope and hauled him back on the ship. By now the man was so terrified he told Drake everything he wanted to know.

According to one account, Drake's fat-cat backers – including Good Queen Bess – received a return of 4,600 per cent, or forty-seven pounds for each pound they had invested. In 1581 Francis Drake was knighted by the queen for his efforts. He was her favourite feller. They'd all had so much fun they decided to do it again.

In 1585 she paid half of the £40,000 costs to send Drake back to South America. As they should have guessed, the Spanish were ready for him this time and he was beaten repeatedly. He returned with just £30,000 in treasure – the queen lost £5,000 and Drake lost 750 men, including some of his best captains.

Even an all-powerful monarch isn't supposed to send high-sea robbers out to attack neutral treasure ships. The Catholic Spanish didn't like Elizabeth and her England too much even before Drake had started plundering their ships. After all, King Philip II of Spain (1527–98) had been married to her big sister Mary.

The trouble with Philip was that he was monarch of an empire that had lands on every known continent. The expression 'the empire on which the sun never sets' was dreamt up during Philip's time, not Queen Victoria's. And because he had such vast swathes of land he was like a trainspotter: he wanted Britannia to complete the set. A little island in the North Atlantic couldn't stand up to his might when his conquistadors were tramping through swathes of South America, could it?

Oddly, he was known as 'Philip the Prudent' when he was anything but. His treasure ships brought fortunes to Spain, yet his misadventures made him bankrupt over and over again. As for his idea that Britannia would be a pushover, that may have been his most imprudent decision of all.

Philip married Maria Manuela of Portugal, but she died shortly after giving birth to his first child, Carlos. Mary Tudor of England ignored this ill omen and agreed to marry him. Their shared passion for the Catholic Church could reinforce the religion's grip in Britain. They met and two days later they married. Mary fell for her new husband; he was less enthusiastic about her. As for the British people, they were very reluctant to have a Spaniard on the throne. He became a prince consort (a bit like Prince Philip in the 1950s when the Brits were unsure about having a Greek on the throne).

After the wedding Phil reported to his sister: 'I was welcomed to England with great demonstrations of affection and general joy.' The words 'wishful' and 'thinking' spring to mind. His

Spanish courtiers were less than courteous about Mary. One wrote: 'The Queen is not pretty, not at all, is low in height, of a fragile structure instead of fat, with very white hair and blonde, has no eyebrows, is holy, she dresses very badly.' They also found the ladies of the court 'pretty ugly'. Hostility to the Spanish visitors crackled in the London air and the feeling was mutual. In London there were several incidents in the street, and Spaniards were often attacked and robbed. Ruy Gomez, a Portuguese noble, reported: 'The king is trying to be as friendly as possible, he believes that his marriage was not made for flesh, but for the restoration of the Spanish states in Flanders.'

With Mary's husband's countrymen keen on the Spanish Inquisition, the English saw its terrors descending on their green and pleasant land. The big-hearted Mary began burning Protestants, despite saying: 'Punishment should be with no cruelty.' The executioners seem to have missed that bit in their instruction book. Anti-Spanish feeling grew.

Philip crossed the Channel on a business trip. He wouldn't return. Mary sent him his favourite pies to lure him back to her arms. They didn't work. Mary had no children and died at the age of forty-two. Her loving husband said: 'I feel a reasonable regret for her death.' How touching. Her Protestant sister, Elizabeth, was waiting in the wings to take the throne. Elizabeth began to persecute Catholics, so they plotted so she persecuted them some more . . . Philip was irritated that 'his' English throne was usurped by this ginger Protestant, and he felt he should take steps to reclaim it.

Philip still had friends in Britannia, so they turned to another Catholic Mary – this one Mary Stuart, Queen of Scots – to help overthrow the red queen. The Spanish planned to invade in the south while the English Catholics rose up to support them. Job's a good 'un. Unfortunately for Mary, Elizabeth had spymasters who knew about most of the plots and got Mary to implicate herself in a scheme to assassinate the queen. Mary had all but signed her own death warrant.* Mary's head was cut off... Well, to be honest, it was chopped and sawn off. Phil was phurious and he decided to go ahead with his invasion even if Mary QoS wasn't around to 'head' a new government.

And so the legendary Armada was born.

In his haste for revenge, Philip was underprepared. If most Brits mistrusted Phil II as king, then their mistrust turned to paranoid hatred when he set out to conquer and convert the nation, and the mighty Armada set sail. The tragicomic tale is quickly told.

Philip was full of hot air but his ships lacked a wind. During the delay the soldiers and sailors aboard ate into their supplies and began to suffer with typhus. Their job was to sail to Flanders, where the Spanish regent, the Duke of Parma, was waiting, then escort the invading fleet across the Channel. Philip fancied himself a great strategist and imposed rules on the Armada officers: they were not to engage the English fleet before meeting up with Parma's force, and they were not allowed to secure an anchorage in England. So, as they sailed past England to Flanders, the Spanish officers reluctantly declined to batter the English in Plymouth where it was vulnerable.

---

* In fact, her cousin Elizabeth signed it and then said she'd changed her mind when it was (conveniently) too late.

The English admiral, Lord Charles Howard, watched the Armada pass so that he could stalk the ships and snipe at the Spanish from the back. Meanwhile, the English Eastern Squadron lay in wait in the Straits of Dover. The English sailors knew the coastal waters well. The English ships were smaller but more efficient – their large guns fired four shots an hour while the Spanish often managed just one. The Spanish admiral began to get his excuses in early. The Duke of Medina Sidonia, in his dispatch of 31 July 1588, said: 'The English continue to harass our rear. Their ships have increased to over a hundred. Some are excellent vessels, and all are very fast sailors. Their ships are so fast and nimble, they can do anything they like with them.'

Phil had bad luck – though the English would say it was fate. The summer of 1588 was one of the stormiest in living memory. As a commemorative Armada medal said: 'Jehovah blew with His winds, and they were scattered.'*

The Spanish oar-and-sail-powered galleasses were fearsome fighters but had weak rudders that sometimes broke down even without English intervention. Two ships collided and one, *Rosario*, damaged her steering. As it was being fixed another ship, *San Salvador*, exploded and blew off its stern. Two hundred Spanish died, along with a lot of the treasure chests that held the wages. Then the *Rosario*, with its shaky steering, managed to collide with yet another ship. An own goal – England 1 – 0 Spain.†

---

* In fact it said it in Latin, '*Flavit Jehovah et Dissipati Sunt*', but you don't need to know that so forget it.
† One conspiracy theory says a German gunner's wife was snuck on board illicitly. When she was molested he blew up the ship in

On 7 August the Spanish reached Calais, searching for Parma and his Flanders troops. The admiral was told that Parma would be ready with the invasion force... in about a fortnight. Meanwhile, the English were preparing to send in fireships to scatter the Spanish fleet. These 'hell-burners' brought terror to the hearts of the Spanish – they'd seen their destructive power earlier in the year at Antwerp. Panic? They were frantic with fear.

As a Spanish eyewitness wrote: 'Eight English ships, with all sail set and a fair wind and tide, came straight towards our fleet, all burning fiercely.' Loaded Spanish cannon began to explode as the fireships reached the galleons. Captains cut the cables on their best anchors and fled. Most evaded the fireships but were carried out into the North Sea with poor replacement anchors, practically useless. Sidonia tried to regroup but it was no use – the tide-swept galleons were scattered.

At daybreak on 8 August the English struck at Gravelines, near Dunkirk. Some Spanish ships had no ammunition left, some sank, and others were driven ashore by hostile winds. A thousand Spanish and a handful of English sailors died.

By 9 August the wind had swung to the south and blew the limping Armada northward up the east coast of England. Discipline among the defeated Spanish was breaking down. Meanwhile, onshore, Parma had heard the news of the Gravelines disaster and abandoned the great plan. A staff officer recalled: 'It was the most fearful day in the world. The whole company had lost hope and foresaw only death.'

---

revenge. Madcap Crazy theory? Yes... except one of the survivors is listed as a German woman.

As the Spanish sailed the long way home – round the north coast of Scotland then down the west coast of Ireland – the English followed like a gamekeeper seeing poachers off the premises, firing the last of their buckshot. The invasion was over, for now. Philip – spitting the sourest of Spanish grapes – could only blame the good old British weather and allegedly said: 'I sent my ships to fight against the English, not against the elements.' But, Philip, if you'd allowed your ships to attack the English fleet in Plymouth then the course of the sea battle – and the history of Britannia – would have changed. We Brits could have been enjoying our summers on the Costa del Bognor as we toasted King Philip XII with sangria.

One of the interesting things about the version of British history you learn in schools is that it presents 'the Armada' as a unique event of the past – like Hastings. They sailed over, we beat them with fireships and a spot of British weather, and then Britannia ruled the waves. But the Armada of 1588 wasn't unique, nor did it put an end to Spanish attempts to conquer the island. W. C. Fields (1880–1946), the US comedian, once said, 'If at first you don't succeed, try, try again. Then quit. There's no point in being a damn fool about it.' Well, Philip was a damn fool.

Philip sent a second Armada in October 1596. You might argue that he *did* change his tactics, as he timed his invasion for a month that is invariably stormier than the 1588 attack. The English fleet struck at Spanish ports and delayed Armada 2 but couldn't stop it. Philip had a bit of luck in that most of the English ships were in dock being refitted – in a season of storms it made sense. He had a clear run at goal. But God sent one of Her gales (again). Déjà vu. Thirty Spanish ships sank, and the rest were driven back to Spain. This time he would surely learn.

Nope.

In 1597, Armada 3 sallied forth to beat the English with a new plan. It was mid-October, again. This time, the plan was that Philip's fleet would take Falmouth while the majority of the English fleet was away in the Azores hoping to destroy the Spanish Atlantic fleet and attack their treasure ships – another open goal. Falmouth would be the base from which the Spanish could sail out and ambush the returning fleet. Third time lucky with the gales? No. Armada 3 was still thirty miles from Falmouth when a gale wrecked twenty-eight ships and drove the rest back home. It was déjà vu all over again.

At this point, Philip did the shrewd thing and died. He had once confided to a Venetian ambassador that he felt he was cursed because he had committed a deadly sin in fancying Princess Elizabeth while he was married to her sister Mary. Maybe a gale blew him away from the gates of heaven.

In 1601, Philip's son decided to avenge his father and Armada 4 was launched. It succeeded. Succeeded in landing in Ireland to support the Earl of Tyrone's rebellion. The trouble was, Tyrone's rebellion failed and the Spanish surrendered.

God saved Her breath that time. She probably didn't have a lot left by then.

War with Spain resumed as early as 1616. It took place largely in Central Europe, so it's seen as a footnote in the history of Britannia. The Protestants were fighting the Catholics again: the next Thirty Years' War was one of the most brutal and destructive wars ever. There were eight million deaths, not only from the battles but also from violence, famine and plague, meaning that the rival nations lost between 25 and 40 per cent of their populations. Cities became empty, smouldering shells. Agriculture took a generation to recover. The Swedish Army alone destroyed fifteen hundred German towns, eighteen thousand villages and two thousand castles.

As in the First World War three centuries later, Britain was part of the war, but was protected by its moat against the miseries of 'less happier lands'. The people of Europe, by contrast, suffered bubonic plague again. Pestilence, War, Famine, Death. Four horses of the Apocalypse. A full house. Britain was largely immune. The Thirty Years' War finally ended, but Britannia never really enjoyed a trusting relationship with Spain.

Eventually, the two naval powers made a deal over the issue of slavery. A series of contracts called *asientos* (assent) were signed by which British merchants were licensed by Spain to sell a quota of slaves to the Caribbean. In the 1713 *asiento* Great Britain held a thirty-year right to send unlimited slaves and five hundred tons of goods to Spanish ports in the Caribbean. That allowed British traders (and smugglers) access to the Spanish markets in America. Anything traded outside the *asiento* contract would be confiscated. The British public – never great fans of Spain – were miffed. When another state of war was declared they celebrated. Prime Minister Sir Robert Walpole (in power 1721–42) snapped: 'They are ringing their bells, soon they will be wringing their hands.'*

Wars can start explosively, but the next conflict with Spain was a slow burner. Eight years slow, in fact. In 1729 Spain

---

* A very early demonstration of a British politician producing a neat sound bite for the voters.

demanded 'stop and search' rights on British vessels, a police tactic that causes bitterness to this day. In 1731 it flared, then died away to a gentle smoulder, like a long fuse inching its way towards a powder keg. The British brig *Rebecca* was boarded by the Spanish coastguard boat *La Isabela*. Spanish commander Juan de León Fandiño accused *Rebecca*'s captain, Robert Jenkins, of smuggling and in the ensuing scuffle Jenkins' ear was hurt (or maybe it was cut off; historians can't agree). The confrontational Fandiño added a threat: 'Go, and tell your king that I will do the same, if he dares to do the same.'*

The outrage appeared to be forgotten. Just another sailors' scrap. It was seven more years before Jenkins was ordered to testify before Parliament. Some reports say that Jenkins produced the severed ear as part of his hearing (is that the right word in the circumstances?). It was pickled in a bottle. The Case of the Severed Ear was just one of several Spanish atrocities being examined by Parliament. Together they were seen as insults to Britain's honour and a clear provocation to war.

Three British warships attacked a Spanish port in Venezuela on 22 October 1739. Note the date. Britain declared war on Spain on 23 October 1739. Whatever happened to famous British 'fair play'? And worse; the British squadron entered the Venezuelan harbour while *flying Spanish flags*. How underhand is that? Fair-play believers will be pleased to know that the Spanish defenders weren't fooled and battered the Brits. Serves the devious chaps jolly well right, don't you think?

---

* To which Jenkins' reply had to be 'Eh?'.

Spain appointed the battle-hardened Don Blas de Lezo to command its defences. Don Blas had lost his left eye and the use of his right arm battling pirates around the world. His left leg was blown off by a cannonball in 1704. By comparison, the British colonists in America were amateurs. They sent two thousand men to attack a Spanish fort. When they got there they discovered their ladders were too short. They took a beating. Britannia wouldn't rule the waves without a lot more fighting.

A hundred years later Thomas Carlyle came up with a name for this phase of Anglo–Spanish hostilities: he called it the War of Jenkins' Ear, and the name stuck. But for every hero there is a cynic or ten. The reputation of heroic Jenkins has not escaped, and the story persists that Jenkins lost his ear in a pub brawl. Still, it's one of the most famous ears in history.

Today Britain's occupation of Gibraltar continues to inflame the Spanish nationalists like a match to a galleon's cannon. One day a new Anglo–Spanish conflict may drive the British apes off the Rock. A dozen British sailors may lose a dozen or more ears in a cod war against Spanish trawlers. The British Empire may last for a thousand years, but school textbooks will still say, 'Gloriana's Armada was their finest hour.' It's hard to imagine any future conflict (which of course will be fought by drones and AI-guided missiles) that could replace the Elizabethans' Armada in the Pride of Britain top-ten victories.

The Spanish Armada has given the English a unifying bond for centuries. Myths evolved as myths do. It was said that Drake was so laid-back he finished his game of bowls before he set off after the Spanish. (He didn't.) Queen Elizabeth said she went to Tilbury to join her soldiers and die among them. (She only went there *after* the storms had dispersed the Spanish fleet.) Elizabeth made a rousing speech about how she had 'the body of a weak and feeble woman; but I have the heart and stomach of a king, and of a king of England too'. (That eloquent speech was first recorded forty years after it allegedly happened.)

The glorious myths fail to mention that when the soldiers were sent home, many joined the unemployed. The sailors suffered worse. The commander of the English fleet, Lord Effingham, wrote to the queen's counsellors to say:

> Sickness and mortality begins wonderfully to grow amongst us; and it is a most pitiful sight to see, how the men, having no place to receive them into here, die in the streets. I am driven myself, of force, to come a-land, to see them bestowed in some lodging; and the best I can get is barns and such outhouses; and the relief is small that I can provide for them here. It would grieve any man's heart to see them that have served so valiantly to die so miserably.

In Gloriana's victory, the sufferings of the men who defeated the Armada could be forgotten; their stories, too, are scattered on the wind.

6

THE DUTCH EMPIRE

Think of the Dutch and you may think of clogs and tulips, cheese and a little boy who saved his country by sticking his finger in a dyke. (Don't try this at home.) That area was part of the medieval Holy Roman Empire and control of what we now call the Netherlands shifted constantly. It must have made the clogs dance with confusion. Then those Inquisition-loving Catholic Spanish tried to stamp out Protestantism in the region, and the Dutch revolted in what turned out to be Eighty Years' War from 1568 to 1648.

When some sort of peace returned, the region flourished and a worldwide Dutch Empire grew. Its public face was the Dutch East India Company which, like the British mercantile companies, relied on invasion, colonialism and robbing the natives of their resources.

At the same time the British Empire was expanding, and Britain had had an East India Company since 1600. It had begun soon after the Armada was defeated, when the captured Spanish ships and cargoes allowed English voyagers to travel the world in search of riches. The Spanish and Portuguese were masters of intercontinental trade, but Britain had elbowed her way to the trough. The Dutch East India Company was another snout in the swill. Conflict was inevitable, and in the early 1600s English traders often fought their Dutch rivals in the Indian Ocean.

The British East India Company had a quarter of a million people serving in its own armed forces – twice as many as the official British Army. For a hundred years from 1757, it effectively 'ruled' India. Its ships acted like a freelance Royal Navy, striking at rival powers. The British East India Company teamed up with the Dutch to attack Spanish ships off the coast of China, so that they could build their trading ports in China free of Spanish influence. But it was the Dutch that had the richest trading company and the jealous Brits went to war with them four times between 1652 and 1784.

The British East India Company was ruthless and amoral. It became involved in the slave trade from the 1680s and went on illegally till 1834, long after Britain had banned it in 1807. The company seemed to live by its own rules, stopping at nothing to accumulate wealth and power. In China it started selling opium to merchants from the 1770s in return for porcelain and tea. Opioid addiction had spread across China by 1820. The Chinese rulers tried to ban opium in 1796 and 1800, but British merchants went on regardless. This led to the First Opium War in 1839, at the end of which the Chinese were forced to let British merchants sell opium and to grant land to the British, including Hong Kong.*

The rival Dutch East India Company had a fight on its hands. At other times in Britain's history there have been relative

---

* We don't talk about it much in Britain, but in China it is seen as the start of a 'Century of Humiliation'.

goodies and baddies – brave Welsh cobblers against the invading forces of Napoleon, say. But in the battles between the Dutch East India Company and the British East India Company it was baddies versus baddies.

The Dutch baddies were people like Jan Pieterszoon Coen (1587–1629), who ended the Dutch conquest of the Banda Islands in Indonesia by eliminating most of the local population. The Dutch had wanted exclusive rights to the precious nutmeg that came from the islands, but the natives wanted the freedom to sell on the open market since the English were offering more. The Banda wrote to King James I to ask for protection: 'Banda do utterly hate the sight of these Hollanders, sons of Whores, because they exceed in lying and villainy.' But no protection arrived in time to prevent a massacre.

The killing of a Dutch trader gave Coen the excuse to slay thousands, send many more into slavery and leave the rest to starve, carrying out a plan to 'subjugate Banda and populate it with other people'. (Of course he didn't mean 'subjugate': he meant 'eliminate'; and he didn't mean 'other people': he meant 'our people'.) This could have been the unspoken motto of empires from time immemorial. 'Eliminate the natives and populate it with our people.' They didn't always state it as bluntly as Coen, but genocide would become an effective approach to conquest. It was irreversible.

Coen's other policy was equally popular with empire-builders everywhere, summed up as: 'Despair not, spare your enemies not, for God is with us.' Divine sanction – 'God on our side' – has been a universal watchword for slaughters of all nations. Sorry to slash, shoot, burn, hang you, mate, but it's what God wants. As well as denuding eastern peoples of their spices, the Dutch East India Company robbed them of rich artefacts and cultural treasures. They were also adept at engineering mass famines.

Coen depopulated the Banda Islands to such a degree that of around fifteen thousand original residents only a thousand remained by the end, with the rest dead, exiled or taken as slaves. An unknown number of natives jumped to their deaths from the cliffs. James I abandoned them to their fate, though the remaining few Banda Islanders were given shelter on a British island in the region. Suddenly short of workers, the Dutch imported slaves from China and India to labour on the plantations alongside the Banda people who had been enslaved. The conditions were so harsh that only a hundred or so of the natives were alive sixty years later.

He would eventually die of cholera, but Coen was long revered as a hero of the Dutch with the usual statues, streets and even a town named after him. The French biologist Jean Rostand (1894–1977) summed it up neatly when he said, 'Kill one man, and you are a murderer. Kill millions of men, and you are a conqueror. Kill them all, and you are a god.'

Places like the Banda Islands could be crushed. Britain would be a tougher nutmeg to crack. In 1623 the tensions between Dutch and British East India Company traders turned nasty when ten Englishmen in Indonesia were beheaded for spying. One English head ended up on a pole, which was quite medieval. Rumours spread that the dead men had been tortured after their arrest. One method was what we would call 'waterboarding' today, but more fanciful reports said they'd been stretched on a rack, burnt and stabbed and (most unusually) had limbs blown off by gunpowder.

The British were furious and the whole country was united in a hatred of the Dutch that would last for almost two hundred years. The Dutch held a show trial of the torturers and found them not guilty (of course). The British East India Company retaliated by publishing a brochure that contained details of the tortures. That wound up the British people to a fever pitch and led to the First Anglo–Dutch War.

The Protestant Dutch had been fighting against the evangelical Catholic Spanish armies with help from the Royal Navy. Now, the Dutch fleets had grown powerful enough to threaten other European powers single-handed. They even had the nerve to use their naval skills to catch more herring in the North Sea than the simple English fishermen. And, of course, they continued to squeeze the British East India Company out of the vast spice trade profits. The Dutch were not well liked. But every war needs a *casus belli* (that's Latin for excuse). It came in the days of Oliver Cromwell and his Roundhead rulers.

The First Anglo–Dutch war started with a triviality far less bloody than Jenkins' Ear. After the execution of Charles I the Commonwealth passed a law in 1652 which said that if a foreign ship met a British warship the foreign ship had to dip its flag in salute. On 29 May a Dutch convoy near Dover were slow to obey the rule and the Brits opened fire, sinking two Dutch vessels. War followed inevitably in July when Cromwell's government refused to say sorry. The British Navy had a few victories, but more damaging were the attacks by British pirates on Dutch merchant ships. Cromwell's Commonwealth won concessions in the end, but thousands died, all for the sake of a dipping flag.

There were wars going on at home too: the Wars of the Three Kingdoms. Cromwell and his Parliamentarians had been battling the Royalists in England, as well as the Scots (who had seen their beloved Stuart family dethroned) and the Catholic Irish (who were being governed by a Protestant elite). The First Anglo–Dutch War gave many British people a common enemy, but any unity didn't last long because Cromwell died (loud cheers from brutalized Ireland) and eventually Charles II took the throne. And Cheerful Charlie had his own agenda when it came to dealing with the Dutch.

The Dutch Protestants were stuck in endless conflict with the Catholic Spanish. Charlie II was a secret Catholic and had few qualms about doing a deal with Spain. So the old Armada enemies united against a new enemy. That rivalry for the spice trade hadn't been settled by the First Anglo–Dutch War, so of course there had to be a second – a bit like the First and Second World Wars.

It began in 1665 and Britain stormed to victories at sea. At Lowestoft in 1665 Prince James – brother of Charles and the future James II – was in command. He escaped miraculously when Dutch chain shot sliced off the heads of the courtiers standing beside him. Then the Dutch commander was blown to pieces when his ship exploded. The enemy ran out of Dutch courage and retreated. It was the worst defeat in the country's naval history. But they managed to escape with a large part of their fleet intact and 'only' two and a half thousand casualties.

That was followed two years later by the worst defeat in *British* naval history at the Raid on the Medway.* King Charles was spending more money on oranges for his mistress Nell Gwynne than he was on maintaining the navy. A lot of his ships were tucked away in the River Medway, south-east of London, awaiting repair or simply saving on the cost of provisions if they put to sea. The Dutch saw their chance. A raid on a little-known seaway would be tricky, but a couple of English pilots defected to the Dutch. Money may have been involved, since Charlie's sailors hadn't been paid for months or even years. The traitorous pilots led the enemy fleet, picking through the narrow channels of the Medway. It took them five days to reach the British dockyards at Chatham – they advanced in 'jumps' at each high tide.

Thirty British sloops were sent to defend the dockyards but only ten were in place. Where were the others? They had been commandeered by the senior officers to carry their possessions away to safety. These precious possessions included – seriously – Dockyard Commissioner Peter Pett's prized collection of model ships.

Despite the slow progress, the Dutch sailed up the Medway unopposed and burnt or captured thirteen prime ships. They then added insult to injury by towing away the flagship of the English fleet, which was of course named HMS *Royal Charles*. Back in London the other Royal Charles – the one with a crown on his curly wig – saw his commanders lose their heads: rich people fled with their money, fearing the Dutch would sail up the

---

* The historians who name these things decided it wasn't worth the title 'Battle' because it was a bit one-sided.

Thames. About thirty Royal Navy ships were deliberately sunk by the English themselves to keep them out of the hands of the Dutch. Poet Andrew Marvell poked fun at the suicide ships:

> Of all our navy none should now survive,
> But that the ships themselves were taught to dive

Rumours spread that the French would be joining in with an invasion fleet. The famous diarist Samuel Pepys was secretary of the Navy Board, and he wrote that there was some good news:

> News is strong that not only the Dutch cannot set out a fleet this year, but that the French will not, and that he Louis XIV hath given the answer to the Dutch Ambassador, saying that he is for the King of England's having an honourable peace, which, if true, is the best news we have had a good while.

Pepys later added that it could mean the start of a revolution against the monarchy. 'The truth is, I do fear so much that the whole kingdom is undone.' The Catholics were the butt of the blame game. Pepys had survived the Great Plague of 1665 and Great Fire of London of 1666 the year before the Raid on the Medway. But the threat of the Dutch was just as depressing: 'Thus in all things, in wisdom, courage, force, knowledge of our own streams, and success, the Dutch have the best of us, and do end the war with victory on their side.'

HMS *Royal Charles* was put on display in Hellevoetsluis in the west Netherlands as a tourist attraction and a reminder of

Anglo-humiliation. An honourable peace was all that was left for Cheerless Charlie.

As well as the Catholics, Peter Pett was blamed. He was asked why he had saved his model ships and not the full-size ships of the fleet. His reply was greeted with disbelieving laughter: 'Because the models were much more valuable.' His argument was that the models were the blueprints for new ships to be built. Hmmmm. Nice try, Pete. He was fined and sacked but had enough wealth to live out his days in comfort. (We do not know what happened to his model ship collection.)

Andrew Marvell plumbed poetic depths deeper than the sunken naval ships with his poem about Pett:

Who to supply with powder did forget
Languard, Sheerness, Gravesend and Upnor? Pett.

A spiteful poem aimed at an easy victim. You might almost say petty.

All this irritated Charlie more than itching powder under his wig. He wanted revenge. It was England 1 – 1 Dutch Republic. Charles wanted to play a decider.

By 1672 the Royal Navy fleet had been rebuilt after the disaster at the Medway. But that disaster was not forgiven or forgotten by Charles II. His people had less of an appetite for an away match. However, the king had signed a treaty with France that guaranteed them mutual support – a bit like the nations of NATO today. When Louis XIV went to war with the Dutch, Charles was obliged by the treaty to send ships and men to help.

In 1673 the Anglo-French fleets penned the Dutch in their ports. The future James II of Britain and his future son-in-law, who would become William III of Orange, commanded the rival fleets though neither took an active part in the battle. Why risk the lives of sailors (on both sides) to break a safe stalemate? The answer, of course, was money. The Dutch spice fleet was due back from the East Indies and would be a gift to Britain and the Royal Navy. Dutch finances were low, and Will of Orange needed the spice cash. They confronted the French and English fleets in an exhausting battle, the Battle of Texel. The greatest loser was the British Admiral Spragge. When his flagship (Spragge-ship?) had its colours knocked off the mast he had to move to a second ship . . . which also lost its topmast and its flag. Again, Spragge climbed into a rowing boat to hoist his colours on a third ship. He never made it. His little boat was sunk and he drowned. Although the overall battle was indecisive, the spice ships got through to rescue the Dutch finances.

By 1674 the Dutch were proving too strong, the French were losing and the British were grumbling that their allies hadn't been a lot of help at Texel. So many wars have been lost because allies fall out. Parliament told King Charles to throw in the towel.

Fourteen years later in 1688 came the Glorious Revolution which threw King James II off the English throne. (He was too openly Catholic where his brother, Charles II, had been a closet Catholic.) James II was replaced by his daughter Mary. Of course she brought along her little husband, the Dutch Stadtholder William III. She was a large lady and he was a small man. Diarist John Evelyn wrote that 'The King and Queen went to Kensington in a coach drawn by six horses, and returned in the evening, the

King hanging upon the Queen's arm like a bauble.' So recently an enemy, William was not universally trusted, but he didn't stick around for long. While he was riding in Hampton Court Park he fell from his horse. He broke his collarbone in the fall, and medical complications in his asthmatic body led to his death.

Of course, there were the usual conspiracy theorists who said he was poisoned by his enemies. They wanted to see Catholic Scot James II restored. They'd be back in 1715 and 1745 in Jacobite rebellions. Other sources say that William III's horse stumbled on a molehill in 1702, leading to the fall. This event was celebrated by the Jacobites, as they toasted to 'the little gentleman in velvet' – some still raise a glass to the mole responsible for Will's spill.

Moleduggery aside, Stadtholder William's elevation to the British crown had put an end to the Anglo–Dutch conflicts of the 1600s. That peace with the Dutch lasted ninety years until 1781, when the Dutch and British fleets fought again in the Battle of Dogger Bank.

By 1780 the American settlers had revolted against British rule and were fighting sea battles. The Dutch recognized the new United States, just when the Brits thought the Dutch were on their side. The Brits took this as a declaration of war. Then, as we saw in the last chapter, the French revolutionaries went to war with Britain, and Dutch merchants began supplying the French Navy. The ensuing war was a disaster for the Dutch, especially economically. It also confirmed the weakening of power of the Dutch East India Company in the 1700s.

One of the final straws in driving Britain to declare war was that the Dutch gave shelter to privateer John Paul Jones. John Paul was a Scot, but he had gone to America to build their navy. When Britain went to war with America, Jones sailed home – to blast Edinburgh with the cannon on his warship. An old priest, watching from the shore, said: 'God could easily send a wind to blow them away.' What happened next? A storm blew up and drove the American ships away. People said it was a miracle. Maybe God is a Scot.

Although he didn't successfully invade Edinburgh, John Paul Jones's work creating the American Navy made him a hero in the United States and France. He was due to be made French ambassador to Algeria but died before the news of his honoured position reached him. In any case he was redundant when the war ended; bad business decisions and an extravagant lifestyle had eaten into his savings. He felt obliged to live up to his 'hero' image. Vanity costs money and he ran out of it (the money, not the vanity). He was buried in a pauper's grave in Paris. A hundred years later his grave was discovered and his body taken back to the United States. He was given a hero's funeral at the naval school he had done so much to create. Now there is a museum dedicated to him and he is recognized as one of the men who helped America win her independence. But John Paul Jones must have died a lonely and disappointed man, feeling sure that he'd been forgotten by the nation he'd fought for. Edinburgh hero to Parisian zero. A familiar fate for warriors.

For thousands of years, war at sea has created its own heroes and heroines. Some individual names, like John Paul Jones, are remembered, but most have been forgotten. Sea battles aren't marked by war memorials, for obvious reasons. But some sea battles have changed the history of the world. One was at Camperdown.

The Dutch may have lost the fourth (and last) Anglo–Dutch War, but her navy was still a thorn in the side of Britannia's attempts to rule the waves. The Dutch fought for Napoleon's France in the French Revolutionary Wars and on 11 October 1797 took part in one of the most important battles in the history of Britain. If Britain had lost at Camperdown against the Dutch, Trafalgar would never have happened, and today's Brits may be singing the 'Marseillaise' while eating Edam cheese.

Forget Admiral Horatio Nelson and remember Seaman Jack Crawford. Jack sailed off to serve his country. At the Battle of Camperdown his ship was struck by a French cannonball. The flag crashed down to the deck – and a fallen flag was a sign that a ship was beaten. Someone had to climb the shattered mast and nail that flag back on.

Jack offered to go. As French cannon and muskets flew around him, he climbed. The French spotted the lonely figure and turned their fire on him. As he neared the top a musket ball tore through his cheek. Jack climbed onward and upward. He nailed the flag back on to the mast and the ship was saved, the battle was saved, England was saved. All because of a brave sailor from Sunderland at the Battle of Camperdown – Britain's most important sea battle.

Jack came home a hero, and the people of Wearside gave him a fine silver medal. But medals don't buy food and drink. After the war it was hard to find work. Jack was forced to sell the medal to live. When cholera landed on a ship outside his house, it found Jack Crawford in slumland. He was the second person to die of cholera that winter, buried in an unmarked grave. Before cholera left the town another 160 had died horribly.*

Eight years later, Lord Nelson didn't nail any flags to the mast. He really was an unsavoury character. To give but one example, Nelson was a friend of slave traders and wrote, 'While I have a tongue, I will launch my voice against the damnable and cursed doctrine of Wilberforce [the abolitionist] and his hypocritical allies.' Nelson foolishly paraded himself on the deck of his ship in all his glittering awards and was duly shot by an enemy sniper, leaving the British fleet exposed without its commander.

Admiral Lord Nelson was given a state funeral, George III cried for him, the Prince of Wales led the four-hour funeral service attended by thirty-two admirals, over a hundred captains and an escort of ten thousand soldiers. Innumerable monuments and memorials were constructed across the country and abroad – including a mighty column in the centre of London. Nelson comfortably topped a recent poll of the greatest hero in eight hundred years of British military history.

Both Nelson and Jack Crawford were brave men, but lords are

---

* Today you can see Jack's medal – the one he had to sell to eat – returned eventually to Sunderland Museum. Outside the museum is Mowbray Park, where you can see Jack's statue at the top of a small hill.

remembered and peasants are forgotten. An example of what Victorian Prime Minister Benjamin Disraeli called 'Two nations – the rich and the poor.'

It's enough to make a peasant revolt.

The Dutch East India Company had one other important legacy. They had settled South Africa in the 1600s and left behind farmers – in their dialect 'Boers' – who spoke a variant of Dutch called Afrikaans. By the end of the 1800s, the devouring wolf was the British Empire and the Boers feared they'd be next to be swallowed up.

Sure enough, when gold was discovered in South Africa it was swamped by foreigners, mainly British. When the British settlers complained they were suffering prejudice and lack of rights, in 1880 an indecisive First Boer War was fought. This was not technically a war between Britain and the Dutch Republic, but the Netherlands supported the Afrikaans farmers. The conflict ended in stalemate.

Then, in 1895, Cecil Rhodes, the British imperialist, organized a raid into the Transvaal (beyond the River Vaal) to overthrow the Boer government and set up a pro-British one. The raid failed, but Rhodes returned to fight the Second Boer War (1899–1902). It was a bloody war and Britain triumphed with superior firepower over the Boers. They also used scorched-earth tactics and concentration camps to crush the Boers' will to fight. This cost them a lot of support from the British people – for once, the Boer farmers were the underdogs, and Brits love an underdog. A rise in taxes to pay for the war may also have contributed to

British disillusionment. And the class system reared its ugly head, as working-class Brits were called up to fight in greater proportions than the middle and upper classes. The Dutch may at times have united Britain in opposition, but in this war the country was divided, just as Disraeli said, into two nations, the rich and the poor.

7

UNITED STATES

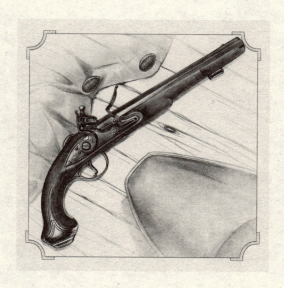

The United States calls itself 'the Land of the Free', apparently without irony. It has also been said (still without irony) that Americans have a fondness for guns. They also have a fondness for eating unhealthy food, electing inane presidents and playing rounders professionally. It's a free country.

The British who settled there became 'free' of British control in the late 1700s. After a civil war against the British establishment in America, they then turned on their old ancestral home and made war on the old country.

Back in 1587, the British colonization of North America had started badly. Queen Elizabeth I sent settlers to claim land and a ship of 114 anchored at Roanoke (now in North Carolina). Their leader, John White, sailed back to Britain for supplies but it was chronically bad timing. Elizabeth was commandeering every ship she could lay her bejewelled hands on to confront the Armada. White finally made it back to Roanoke in 1590. He'd left his wife, daughter and granddaughter (Virginia Dare, the first English child born in the Americas). And there they were: gone. In fact, all 114 of the settlers had disappeared. There was no trace of the colony, and little clue as to what had happened, apart from a single word, 'Croatoan', carved into a wooden post.

(Americans are notoriously bad at spelling so perhaps it was a plea for croutons.) Had they tried to sail home and been lost at sea? Were they abducted by Native Americans – or aliens?

The vanishment didn't deter settlers and another bunch landed at Jamestown, just to the north, seventeen years later. As early as 1619 the first African slaves landed in America. They'd be there long after the trade was banned back in Britannia. Those Jamestown settlers weren't very bright. They dug for gold before they dug in for food. No surprise that they starved, and some lived by eating one of the settler corpses after it had been buried for three days. Others enjoyed gourmet meals of dog, rat, mouse, snake or horse meat. One man murdered his wife and began to eat her. When he started salting away the rest of her to get him through the winter he was caught and hanged. Meanwhile, the Pilgrims set up the Plymouth Colony in Massachusetts. Pilgrim William Mullins took 126 pairs of shoes and thirteen pairs of boots, but no one took a plough or a horse, a cow or even a fishing line. Never mind, the Native Americans they met helped them survive.

In 1632, Maryland was founded as a colony by Lord Baltimore, and thirty years later King Charles II 'granted' a charter to eight English noblemen to set up the Province of Carolina, where King Charles had never set foot. No one thought to ask the Native Americans if the Brits could move in. But the Brits did gift the natives diseases such as smallpox, measles and influenza; even bubonic plague. The Native Americans weren't immune to any of these European maladies. During the 1600s, the Native American population of Virginia declined by around 90 per cent. By 1758 this accidental decimation had become deliberate. The British general Jeffrey Amherst gave his Native American enemies a peace offering. He gave them blankets. Where did he get the gifts from? From the corpses in the British smallpox hospital. It was early biological warfare.

This was not the first sign of friction between the settlers and the locals, either. In 1675 King Philip's War broke out when the Wampanoag chief's son (nicknamed King Philip) tried to rebel against colonizers in New England. Settlers were massacred, and naturally the Wampanoag were massacred back. A soldier reported: 'An Indian woman was ordered to be torn to pieces by dogs, and so she was.' William Bradford had arrived in America on the *Mayflower* and became governor. His diary recorded a similar attack on the Pequots in 1637: 'Those that escaped the fire were slain with the sword. Some were chopped to pieces and some stabbed with rapiers, so they were killed quickly. But it was a fearful sight to see them frying in the fire and the streams of blood putting out the flames. The scent and stink was horrible, but the victory made it seem like a sweet sacrifice. They gave their thanks to God who had created such a wonderful victory.' Brits knew how to deal with enemies – especially enemies with less powerful weapons. King Philip was captured, and his head was stuck on a pole. (God probably received thanks for that too.)

In 1739 black slaves in South Carolina met the same sort of fate when they rebelled by simply walking off towards Spanish Florida and freedom. They killed twenty-one white people they met on the way, but when they came across an army of white settlers the rebels were massacred.

British settlers soon arrived in the Dutch colony of New Amsterdam, pinched it from them and renamed it New York. But don't feel too sorry for the Dutch. When one Dutch farmer was killed by the Wappinger tribe, the Dutch retaliated by massacring the tribe. Everyone died bar one, and he would be left wishing he had been killed quickly. The Dutch castrated him, then they sliced off his skin, cut off pieces of flesh and forced him to eat them. It was reported that the Dutch governor laughed at the sight till tears ran down his face.*

By now the Brits held the east of America, the French the middle and the Spanish the west. It was bound to lead to trouble. In 1762 Spain joined the French to bash the Brits. Two-on-one isn't cricket. A year later a peace treaty left Spain with the west and France with nothing. The Native Americans were squashed in the middle but were promised that the Brits wouldn't move west to take their lands. (So that's all right.)

Tensions were developing between the British back home and the British in the colonies, who whinged that they didn't have the same rights as those in Britannia. The settlers wanted to form their own armies to defend their land-grabs from the French, who were threatening from their bases in Canada, as well as the Native Americans. But the British government argued that if there were going to be armies, Britain would supply them – paid for by a Sugar Tax. Then, when the British Stamp Act of 1765 insisted the settlers buy goods from Britain – *and* pay British taxes on those goods – the colonists were up in arms.

The British sent troops to occupy Boston and quell the unrest. As you can guess, it had the opposite effect. British 'peacekeeping'

---

* The Dutch paid their settlers to kill natives and all they required was a scalp to prove a death. It was the Dutch who popularized the practice of scalping, not the natives.

soldiers in Boston were stoned by a mob and opened fire, killing five Americans. They called it 'the Boston Massacre'. The *New Hampshire Gazette* proclaimed: 'The streets of Boston have been bathed with the blood of innocent Americans.' That may be considered a bit over the top. In truth the rioters asked for it – actually *asked* for it. They gathered round the Redcoats and shouted in their faces, 'Go on, fire! Damn you, you sons of bitches, fire. Why don't you fire?' The soldiers fired and the Bostonians cried, 'Why did you fire?' A couple of Brit soldiers were found guilty of manslaughter and branded on the thumb. But the Americans wanted real revenge.

In 1773 the British government proposed sending cut-price tea to America from the East India Company. The condition was that the settlers didn't buy tea from anyone else. Yet it would still be a real bargain. The British motive was to bail out the struggling East India Company. The EIC's greed – prioritizing trade crops like indigo and opium over food crops that would sustain the Bengalis – had resulted in the Great Bengal Famine of 1770. Two years of bad harvests meant that between seven and ten million indigenous Bengalis starved to death. The EIC 'relief' efforts were late and inadequate. Naturally, EIC revenues declined with the lack of labour.

You may think the British government would have seized the considerable EIC assets to make reparations? Quite the opposite. The government bailed out their tea-trading friends and with the Act of 1773 granted the struggling company the monopoly right to sell its tea in the American colonies, cheaply and to a captive market. The American reaction was the Boston Tea Party, which wasn't really a tea party unless you like tea made with seawater. A group of colonists disguised as Native Americans boarded three British ships and dumped 342 chests of tea into Boston Harbor. The rebels came up with a rebel song, though they clearly couldn't afford a decent poet to pen the lines:

Rally, Mohawks, bring out your axes,
And tell King George we'll pay no taxes
On his foreign tea.
His threats are weak, he's mad to think
He'll force our girls and wives to drink
His filthy tea.

Good to know that the tea-throwers were thinking of the comforts of their girls and wives and not the tax. The British responded with the Coercive Acts, which closed Boston Harbor and placed Massachusetts under military rule.

In 1774 the rebel settlers created their own government, the grand-sounding Continental Congress. They also started to arm themselves. The real shooting started in 1775. At the North Bridge near Lexington, the British Army retreated but a wounded soldier fell into enemy hands. The British general Thomas Gage described what happened next: 'An American youth ran across the bridge and attacked the wounded soldier with an axe. The poor man was scalped, his head was mangled, and his ears cut off while he was still alive.'

The British Army marched on to Concord and the Battle of Bunker Hill left the rebels bloodied but not bowed. They elected the soldier George Washington, a veteran of the wars with French America, to lead their military efforts. By 1776 the British armies were struggling, and the confident Americans made their 'Declaration of Independence'. It was adopted on 4 July, so that's when Americans now have their parties.* (Not tea parties.)

The war was conducted at sea as well as on land. The Americans won a curious victory over the British schooner the *Margaretta*. The crew had anchored in Machias Bay and gone to church. There they were attacked by farmers waving sickles. The British jumped out of their seats and raced back to their ship. Two boat-loads of angry Americans followed them, climbed aboard the *Margaretta* and killed the captain. The crew surrendered.

The British warship *Eagle* was also at anchor when it was the victim of another unusual American attack. It was the first ship to be damaged by a submarine. The little underwater vessel was invented by an American farmer and called *American Turtle*. It looked like a two-metre wooden egg and carried a barrel of gunpowder which was timed to explode soon after it was released under an enemy ship. The torpedo failed to sink the *Eagle* but the sight of it terrified the crew, who chased after the submarine but failed to capture it.

The Brits had tried the tactic of appealing to American slaves, saying that if they joined the British Army they would win their freedom. But two could play at the bribe-your-enemy game. One-third of Georgie's British Army came from Hesse in Germany. These Hessians were mercenaries, so George Washington and his government came up with an offer to pay the Hessian

---

* The 'Declaration of Independence' states that 'all men are created equal'. What they really meant was 'all men are created equal – unless they happen to be Native American or black or female'.

soldiers *not* to fight them. What's more, General Washington was armed with promises of free land to any Hessian soldier who switched sides. (Of course, the land the rebels promised didn't belong to them.) As well as this, the French supplied arms and money. Everything has its price, and the French government would expect American repayment when they went to war with Britain in the Napoleonic Wars.

In 1783 Britain conceded defeat and the Treaty of Paris saw American independence recognized. But the conflict with the new United States of America wasn't over.

By 1812 the United States was finding its feet as a nation and looking to expand. Britain stood in her way. It didn't help that Britain was at war with America's buddy Napoleon and had been press-ganging American seamen to fight for Britain. So in June 1812 the United States declared war.

The first prong of the attack was to send privateers to raid British shipping. They made a good start. The American sloop *Argos* captured twenty-seven ships in raids around the coasts of Britain. Then it met the eighteen-gun HMS *Pelican*, evenly matched in guns and crews. *Argos* could have run away, but Captain William Allen chose to stay and fight. *Argos*'s crew started to lose the gun battle when two things were shot off: the main mast and Captain Allen's leg. *Argos* surrendered.

Some Americans also wanted to expand into British-controlled Canada, but their capture of Toronto in 1813 came at great cost. As they approached the city the British blew up their ammunition store to stop the weapons and explosives falling into the hands of the Americans. The explosion was huge, and a witness reported that 'the sky rained boulders'. (And to think people complain about the rain in Britain.) The next year a British force retaliated with an attack on Washington, where they burnt the White House to a sort of Charcoal-grey House.

The war ended on Christmas Eve 1814, but news didn't reach the southern states of America so the famous Battle of New Orleans took place, where two thousand British soldiers lost their lives. The American general Andrew Jackson had help from the French pirate Jean Lafitte. Lafitte had brought terror to the Bay of Mexico with his fleet of ten pirate ships. He didn't so much sail the seas himself as organize the pirate team, a bit like a football manager who doesn't get his knees dirty. In fact, Lafitte was legendary for being a socialite and having courteous manners.

The French pirate had previously upset the US government and a warrant was put out for his arrest. The Louisiana governor put a price of $750 on Lafitte's head; he responded by putting a $1,500 bounty on the governor's head. No one sold Lafitte out because the traders who knew what he looked like were getting a steady stream of goods at a piratical discount.

As the Battle of New Orleans was brewing, the British offered Lafitte a Royal Navy rank of captain and a sweetener of $30,000 to fight with them. Lafitte declined and went to the New Orleans authorities to see if they'd care to match the British offer. Far from agreeing, the US governor W. C. C. Claiborne did the very opposite and sent a US naval force to attack Lafitte's pirate base. A number of pirate ships in the harbour were captured, but Lafitte and most of his men escaped inland.

But when General Andrew Jackson arrived to command the

defence of New Orleans he decided it was politic to sup with the devil and met with Lafitte. The pirate was granted a pardon and a command, and this force was an important factor in the defence of the city on 8 January 1815. Although the British had a numerically superior force, they were repulsed. Afterwards, all one thousand of Lafitte's men were given a pardon by President James Madison (in office 1809–17). Unfortunately, what Lafitte didn't get back was the proceeds of his crimes before Governor Claiborne had attacked his pirate ships. That may have driven him back into a life of crime once the war was over.

His attacks on Spanish ships were ignored by the US authorities. But when he turned his thieving ways to US ships – stealing arms and slaves – the United States sent a warship to deal with him. Lafitte claimed one of his men was responsible and had the man hanged. That satisfied the authorities and the pirate sailed off into the sunset (or at least into legend). No one knows what happened to him.

From the pirate John Paul Jones in the earlier conflicts to Jean Lafitte in New Orleans, the United States got an early taste for hiring mercenaries to fight their wars. As for the British, they had a lot on their minds. They were already fighting Luddites at home and enemies in Spain and France. The US wars of 1812 to 1814 weren't seen as a crusade that united the Brits. At the same time, they were a significant event in American history, helping to forge a sense of national unity and identity in the United States. Already, the United States was a military force to be reckoned with.

The United States used its newly confident military to drive the Native Americans ever westward, then to near-extinction. In

1846 American forces gave the Native Americans a break and attacked the Mexicans instead. A commentator at the time said: 'It is one of the most unjust wars ever waged against a weak nation.' Who said that? US General Ulysses Grant! Still, just or unjust, it was profitable: the United States won half a million square miles of new land.

The British Empire-builder Cecil Rhodes was deluded enough to believe that Britain could expand its empire till it ruled the whole world. He said: 'Why should we not form a secret society with but one object, the furtherance of the British Empire and the bringing of the whole world under British rule.' This object also included a plan 'for the recovery of the United States, for making the Anglo-Saxon race but one empire. What a dream, but yet it is probable; it is possible.'

No, Cecil, it never was possible, but Britain does have a 'special' bond with the United States, reinforced by having a common enemy in two world wars. In both, the Americans hung back until it suited them to join on the side of Britain and her Allies. The First World War accelerated the United States' rise as an industrial power and the industrialists profited, allowing eight thousand Americans to become millionaires.* Of course, the workers faced rising costs of living and stagnant wages.

In the Second World War many more joined the US millionaires club. After the Second World War came the Marshall Plan,

---

* A million dollars in 1914 would be about $30 million today. The world also saw its first billionaire, John D. Rockefeller, whose oil wealth soared.

a loan named after George Marshall, the US secretary of state who proposed it in 1947. The Marshall Plan was aimed at helping Western Europe recover from the devastation of the war. The United States provided over $15 billion in aid to rebuild factories, infrastructure and economies. In hundreds of raids the US Air Force had destroyed the infrastructure the Marshall Plan was designed to remedy. So the United States wrecked German cities and then loaned them money to rebuild them.

Britain took sixty years to pay off its Marshall Plan loan after the Second World War. The final payment was made in December 2006. Two centuries previously, a war against the US enemy had been costly. Now, a war with the United States as an ally left countries like Britain financially and morally 'in debt' to the United States . . . and no one wants to upset their bank manager.

8

RUSSIA

Russia: snow to freeze you and vodka to warm you up again. Lousy Lada cars and lousier KGB spies. After centuries of tsars with their Fabergé eggs, Communism levelled the playing field. Now everyone is a peasant. That's levelling up for you.

In fairness, you might think twice about having a tsar if they were as cruel as Ivan IV, aka Ivan the Terrible (tsar from 1547 to 1584). He was married eight times, putting even Henry VIII in the shade. Wife number five, Anna Vasilchikova, found herself a new boyfriend, but Ivan found out. The lucky woman was packed off to a nunnery, but not before the boyfriend was stuck on a spike and left to die outside Anna's palace window. Ivan's seventh wife, Maria Dolgorukaya, lasted the shortest time of all. Like Henry VIII's Catherine Howard, Maria had had another boyfriend the monarch didn't know about. When Ivan found out he had his new bride drowned. They were married for one day. Ivan's treasurer Nikita Funikov was boiled alive, while his enemy Prince Boris Telupa was spiked on a wooden pole – he took fifteen hours to die and talked through it to his mother, who was being forced to watch. Ivan would lash out at people who annoyed him with a heavy sceptre. One day he lashed out at his own son and killed him. Deadly sort of dad to have.

All of this was happening at the same time Mary Tudor was burning Protestants before her sister Elizabeth was torturing Catholics to death and, up in Scotland, Mary Queen of Scots was blowing up her husband. The British and the Russian royals of the 1500s and 1600s were clearly kindred spirits. In fact, when Tsar Alexei heard about the Roundheads executing Charles I in 1649, he was furious. He expelled all English traders and residents from Russia to demonstrate solidarity with Charlie. (Too late, of course, for Charles to appreciate the gesture.)

Alexei's son, Tsar Peter I of Russia (reigned 1682–1721), visited his royal friends in London from 1697 to 1698 and while there he was invited to the Tower of London. He must have picked up a few handy tips from the torture chambers there. After a stay of 105 days, he hurried back to Russia when news of a military rebellion broke. Peter wanted in to make a public demonstration of punishments on the elite military who had rebelled against him. Many suspects were whipped to death with a brutal instrument known as a knout. The knout was usually made of leather thongs that were attached to a long wooden handle. The thongs were often twisted together and could be tipped with metal hooks. It would be handled by a skilled executioner, who could deliver powerful blows that would tear the flesh from the victim's body.* Other rebels were stretched until their limbs broke; iron thumbscrews were used on the fingers of many suspects, while

---

* The knout was eventually abolished in Russia in 1904.

some had their backs slowly roasted. The unlucky ones had their fleshy parts and feet nipped with red-hot iron pincers.

Britain's official policy at this time was not to worry too much about what was going on elsewhere. The priority was to sustain the riches of the empire and not to be bound by treaties with other great powers – a policy that would eventually come to be known as 'Splendid Isolation'. The Brits also wanted to maintain the 'Balance of Power' so that no single nation became the bully of Europe. This meant Russia and Britain fought on the same side during the War of the Austrian Succession (1740–48), but on opposite sides during the Seven Years' War (1756–63). They didn't actually meet on a battlefield in either. The two countries became allies against Napoleon in the early 1800s, but by the 1850s they had found a reason to engage in a bitter war – the Crimean War. The next few years were not so Splendid.

Power in the world shifts like sand dunes in a storm. The Ottoman Empire lasted longer than most (1299 to 1922 to be exact). It was centred around what's now Greece and Turkey, then took in swathes of the Mediterranean coast, from the Levant to North Africa. But gradually the empire was weighed down by internal squabbles, wars and economic troubles. The wolves were gathering at the edges.

Britain and France gave the excuse that the Muslim Ottoman rulers were controlling the Christian Holy Lands. A dispute over a shrine in Bethlehem led to Christian and Muslim conflict. It was the Crusades revisited. The Russians portrayed themselves as the protector of Orthodox Christians, marching into the Ottoman lands around the Black Sea. France saw itself as the protector of Roman Catholics – and also saw the Russian move as a threat to its trade routes. Russia's actions were hitting Britain in the wallet, so both Britain and France said they would support the Ottomans. They declared war on Russia in March 1854.

The war was only possible because of the Industrial Revolution: Britain had steam-powered ships to get armies and supplies to and from the Black Sea, as well as fancy new weapons like rifled muskets. British public support was mixed: a great chance to uphold British interests against Russian aggression, said the hawks; a waste of lives and money, said the doves. But the acts of heroism were almost universally admired.

The Times originated the practice of sending war correspondents to cover conflicts. W. H. Russell wrote immensely influential dispatches on the Crimean War; for the first time, the public could read about the reality of warfare even as it was happening. Russell wrote one dispatch that highlighted the surgeons' 'inhumane barbarity' and the lack of ambulance care for wounded troops. Prompting shock and outrage, the public backlash led to major reforms especially in the provision of nursing, led by Florence Nightingale.

The Lady with the Lamp. It's one of two images of the Crimean War that have remained in the national consciousness through school history lessons, as the rest has faded. Florence Nightingale's name is an anagram for 'Flit on cheering angel'. Very appropriate. As a (rather sentimental) 1913 biography of her claimed: 'She is a "ministering angel" without any exaggeration in these hospitals, and as her slender form glides quietly along each corridor, every poor fellow's face softens with gratitude at the sight of her. When all the medical officers have retired for the night and silence and darkness have settled down upon those miles of prostrate sick, she may be observed alone, with a little lamp in her hand, making her solitary rounds.'

Florence was a posh kid who heard God calling her to do something good, so she led a team of nurses to help the sick British soldiers dying of disease in the Crimean War. Her real talent was statistics and presenting them in graph form (like pie charts), which helped her reach insights and plan logistics that would save lives. The ordinary soldiers were suffering and dying from disease (especially cholera) as much as from their wounds. In the hospitals they were lying on dirty floors two weeks before they got to see a doctor. Those floors were crawling with rats and insects. The men had no beds, and some had no blankets or pillows – they rested their heads on their boots. There were no toilets, just twenty chamber pots for a thousand men in one hospital, and the pots overflowed. All that changed with the arrival of Florence Nightingale and her team of almost forty nurses. Soon they reduced the deaths by two-thirds.

Later, she fell ill and blind for so long she took more nursing than she gave out. Recent commentators have said that Florence's Crimean War achievements were exaggerated by the media at the time in order to boost morale when the war was looking like endless misery. But even her critics agree that the creation of a professional nursing career for women owes everything to her. Before Florence, nursing as we know it now did not exist. The critic Lytton Strachey regarded her as an intense, driven woman who was both personally intolerable while being admirable in her achievements. Probably not the epitaph she'd have wanted.

The other seminal moment in the war was the Charge of the Light Brigade. People who can't put a finger on Crimea on a map can quote lines from the Tennyson poem that glorified the typical British quality of plucky failure:

> 'Forward, the Light Brigade!'
> Was there a man dismayed?
> Not though the soldier knew
> Someone had blundered.
> Theirs not to make reply,
> Theirs not to reason why,
> Theirs but to do and die.
> Into the valley of Death
> Rode the six hundred.

In 1854, at the Battle of Balaclava, the allies had hoped to gain control of the port and fortress of Sevastopol but were hampered by the Russian Army. During this indecisive battle a misinterpreted order led to the Charge.

The commander ordered the Light Brigade to stop the Russian enemy taking away the cannon of the Turkish allies. The message reached the Earl of Lucan, who couldn't actually *see* the Turkish guns in question. He turned to the messenger, Captain Nolan, and said, 'What guns?' Nolan waved his arm in a wide sweep that seemed to indicate the Russian guns. He would be killed in action – which probably served him right, because over 150 men would die with another 120 wounded. That's quite apart from the horses, who probably didn't want to be there. In a battle between cavalry and cannon there is only going to be one winner.

Lord Cardigan led the attack on his horse, Ronald. Seeing the error of his sweeping gesture, Captain Nolan rushed in front of

Ronald to cry something like, 'No-o-o. Sorry. My bad.' We'll never know exactly what he intended to say because a shell blew him away. The Light Brigade rode on. One of the survivors, Captain Godfrey Morgan, summed up the horror: 'I appeared to be riding straight on to the muzzle of one of the guns, and I distinctly saw the gunner apply his fuse. I shut my eyes then, for I thought that settled the question as far as I was concerned. But the shot just missed me and struck the man on my right full in the chest.'

Within six weeks the poet Alfred Tennyson had churned out a heroic poem that made the stupidity of the army look like a glorious action. It predated the other heroism-against-the-odds poem 'Play up! play up! and play the game' by forty years (a poem which would convince a different bunch of young men to march to their deaths in a different war).

The Crimean War was bloody and costly, with over six hundred thousand soldiers killed in total, more from cold and disease than enemy action. In the end the allies defeated Russia, and Russia was forced to cede territory to the Ottoman Empire and to demilitarize the Black Sea. But by the end of the conflict, most Britons were opposed to the war and saw it as a failure.

Russia and Britain sniped at one another for control of Central Asia in the latter half of the 1800s but they never erupted into a full-scale war again. The rivalry between Britain and Russia became known as 'the Great Game'. For 355 dead horses at Balaclava, they may have preferred polo.

In the First World War the Russians fought on the side of the Allies against Germany. Tsar Nicholas II took charge of the army himself, and as you'd expect things got worse. The Russian people blamed Nick for the horrors the enemy inflicted on them, so they had a revolution, and Communist rebels took over the country.

The tsar had suffered a minor revolt in 1905 after a disastrous war against Japan and the royals had to cede some democratic power to the people. The Russian royals were related to many other royal families, thanks to Queen Victoria's proclivity for arranging marriages of her nine children across Europe. Nicholas was a pleasant sort of bloke and popular with his relatives, such as his cousin George V of England. In 1917, as order broke down, Nicholas went to the front line to confront the revolutionaries – the Bolsheviks – while his wife and children were urged by the government to flee. Loyal Alexandra refused to leave without Nicholas; he abdicated so that he could return to his family.

George V wrote private letters of support for the Russian royals, but his own future was uncertain. Most Brits at the time called the ex-tsar 'Bloody Nicholas' for his violent treatment of protestors in 1905. Peaceful strikers were carrying his image when they were shot down by the Imperial Guard. Thousands were wounded and killed, earning him the 'Bloody' handle. The German-born Alexandra was viewed with even greater suspicion.

Opposition to sheltering the Russian royals was a unifying force in Britain. And of course, the British needed to stay friendly with the Bolsheviks. After all, the Russian Eastern Front was weakening the German war effort against France and Britain on the Western Front. Upset the Bolsheviks and the Germans could turn their full firepower on the Allies. But in an unexpected twist, the new Russian government *asked* Britain to give Nick and his family asylum. The longer he stayed in Russia, the more chance there was of a counter-revolution to restore the royals. Britain said 'yes', then mysteriously rescinded the offer. Who blocked the offer of refuge to George V's cousin? George himself: his secretary had scared the king with predictions of a British revolution.*

Nick and his family were placed under house arrest and eventually sent to Ipatiev House in a remote place called Yekaterinburg. Ipatiev House was known as 'the House of Special Purpose', and that special purpose wasn't a retirement home. The Communists knew that an army of royal supporters were gathering to rescue the royal family, so they had to die – the whole line. But massacres can be messy.

In the early hours of the morning on 17 July 1918, the royal family were woken up, told to dress, and taken to the basement. An officer assured them that they were being moved for their own safety as there could be some shooting. (This is rather like the dentist telling you, 'This won't hurt.') Nicholas had Alexandra and their five children with him, along with their doctor and three of their servants.

A firing squad of seven entered the room, and their commander told the tsar that they were sentenced to death. Nicholas cried out 'What? What?' in disbelief. The soldiers pulled out

---

* If you want to excuse George V's cowardly act you could point out that Nick's other relatives in Norway, Denmark, Spain and Sweden all got equally cold feet.

pistols and the killing began. Nicholas was the first to die. His four daughters, Anastasia, Tatiana, Olga and Maria, lived through the first hail of bullets; they were wearing over 1.3 kilos of diamonds and other jewels sewn into their clothes. They were stabbed with bayonets and then shot at close range in the head, the bodies mutilated with grenades to prevent identification before they were buried in an unmarked grave.

After the slaughter, only Nicholas' death was revealed at first. The British royals held out hope of saving the children and so, once the war was over, the British sent a ship to evacuate the remaining minor royals. The phrase 'too little, too late' must have haunted George V to his grave.

The Communists finally lost power in 1989. In 1977, as the sixtieth anniversary of the revolution approached, a local party apparatchik named Boris Yeltsin had the house destroyed. The murdered family would only get a proper burial in 1998.

The new Communist leader in 1917 was Vladimir Ilyich Ulyanov, better known to history as Lenin. What did Lenin have against the tsars? It was personal. Lenin's older brother, Alexander, had been arrested for plotting to bomb the tsar, also called Alexander (II). In 1881 rebels had attacked the tsar's carriage. A bomb wrapped in newspaper was thrown in front of it and that killed the horses and two guards. Alex got out to see how they were. He was very fond of horses. A man in the crowd called, 'Are you all right?' and Alex said, 'Yes . . . thank God.' The bomber cried, 'It's too early to thank God' as he threw a second bomb which tore holes in Alex's legs and chest. Still all right, Alex? No. He died, and the other Alexander was hanged.

Lenin was accused of helping his brother plot a revolution and was sent away to a prison camp in Siberia to cool off. Prisons have long been seen as incubators for radicalism and, sure enough, Lenin met other Communist plotters there. When he was set free, he began preaching revolution throughout Europe and went to other potentially sympathetic cities like Manchester. But Manchester city wasn't united, and he moved on.

The First World War was probably the best thing that ever happened to Lenin. Three years in, the Russian people were battered and starved by the war and ready for radical change. Lenin stuck a wig on his bald head and shaved off his goatee so he could sneak back into Russia. After seizing power, Lenin set up the Secret Police to execute anyone who got in his way. Naturally, there were lots of plots to kill him and one was bound to succeed. In 1918 he was shot. He lived, but the wounds left him weak, and one bullet stayed in his neck. He died six years later.

If the French Revolution had their 'Reign of Terror' then Lenin had his 'Red Terror', with bullets instead of guillotines. Some say two hundred and eighty thousand died. It made the French Reign of Terror look like a Reign of a-bit-of-a-fright. Compared to the next Russian leader, Joseph Stalin, Lenin was just a beginner: at least twenty million, and possibly as many as sixty million, died during his dictatorship.

Hundreds of years of monarchy in Britain and Russia had been a bond. Now that was gone, Russia was no longer a natural ally of Britain. In 1939, Stalin signed an agreement with Adolf Hitler to divide parts of Europe between them as war with France and Britain loomed. In exchange neither country would attack the other. Hitler broke the pact in 1941 with his invasion of Russia, known as Operation Barbarossa. It was the largest military operation in history, involving more than three million German soldiers and over three thousand tanks. It was also a huge German mistake, and one of the major reasons why Germany eventually lost the war. The Soviet Union won the Eastern Front again, at a great cost of maybe twenty-seven million Soviet citizens.

When the war was over the principal Allies, France, the United States and Britain, had a mutual distrust of Russia, which was really only their enemy's enemy. Winston Churchill said it was as if an 'Iron Curtain' had descended to separate Russia and its satellite states from the rest of Europe. A 'Cold War' had begun and, as nuclear weapons proliferated, there was an ever-present fear that it could turn into an all-consuming hot one. By this time Stalin's successor, Nikita Khrushchev, perceived Britain as a toothless sheep, but was kind enough to offer advice: 'If you live among wolves you have to act like a wolf.'

Thanks, Nikita.

It was mistrust of Russia that persuaded Britain, the United States and their allies to flock together in a way they had never done before, sharing intelligence, foreign policy and even joining one another's wars. Unity in the face of the Russian bear was true after the Second World War and remained true when President Vladimir Putin invaded Ukraine in 2022. As Khrushchev also said: 'The USA and USSR will only agree when shrimps learn to fly.'

9
IRELAND

Fabled land of rain and shamrocks, potatoes and Guinness, religion and leprechauns, and dancing on rivers. It is also the land of the most euphemistic of euphemisms ever: 'the Troubles'.

Some historians are especially nasty when it comes to writing about Ireland. The Irish writer Geoffrey Keating complained about English historians who focus on the less savoury aspects of Ireland's past: 'The English historian is like a dung beetle. He ignores the garden flowers and the sweet-smelling blossom. Instead, he keeps bustling about until he meets the dung of a cow or a horse and starts to roll about in it.' Give a dog a bad name and it will live up to it (or down?).*

Humans settled in Ireland twelve thousand to fourteen thousand years ago, and by the Stone Age (around 4000 BC) had settled into cultures that built sophisticated 'passage tombs' at

---

* Geoff, who was writing four hundred years ago, allegedly paid heavily for his disrespectful comments about English historians – Irish historians said Geoff was killed by one of Cromwell's soldiers. But Cromwell rampaged through Ireland from 1649 and Geoffrey died in 1644. Who's the bad historian now?

Newgrange, Knowth and Dowth, older even than Stonehenge or the Egyptian pyramids. Ireland led the way in engineering and craftsmanship. The passages align with the solstices, so their astronomy was pretty good too.

The Celts, whom we met in the first chapters, arrived around 500–300 BC and would stay in power for a thousand years – Ireland wasn't occupied by the Romans in the way England was. By the AD 400s the Irish were organized into six kingdoms, with a warrior class defending (or attacking) at their king's bidding.

The pope sent his first missionary, Palladius, to Ireland in 431. He's forgotten now because a year later St Patrick followed in his holy sandals and would be remembered evermore, his saint's day celebrated from Dublin to Boston. Speaking of sandals, there's a tale about St Patrick and King Aengus's foot. Pat was blessing the king with his crozier (a rod topped by a cross) when he accidentally brought down the pointy end on the king's foot. The king took the pain without complaint, maybe imagining it was part of the ceremony. But don't worry about the agony of Aengus – the saint healed the foot with one of his miracles.

By 563, Ireland was exporting Christianity to the heathens in Scotland and England in the person of St Columba. Some chronicles say he was no saint: he may have started a tribal war back in Ireland in which five thousand died. The facts about Columba's life are mixed with legends, like the story that he was a skilled poet and had a voice that could be heard a mile away, or the myth that he once killed a wild boar with the power of his words. He even defeated a 'water beast' in Loch Ness with his prayers, the first written encounter with the Monster. The memory of Columba shouting at her could be why Nessie is so reluctant to raise her head above the waters these days.

The Irish loved their saints, from Kevin (who lived up a tree) to Brendan (who enjoyed a chinwag with angels) or Brigid (who changed bath water into beer – it's not clear whether she had bathed in it first). St Kentigern may have lived to 185, or that could have been a typo that the primitive spell-checkers of the monastic Middle Ages failed to pick up on. The monastic system also created the first free hospitals – a sort of prototype National Health Service.

They weren't all pacifists. What would St Patrick have said when two hundred monks were killed in a war between two monasteries? In the year 764, men from the community of Durrow went to battle against those of Clonmacnoise. Later, the death toll in this battle was exceeded by a bloody war in 817 between the monasteries of Taghmon and Ferns, in which four hundred were killed. The monastic vows insisted on the monks living according to the rules of poverty, chastity and obedience. Maybe those rules should have said something about brotherly love? Still, it was good practice for resisting the Vikings when they arrived in 795 and started desecrating monasteries. The monks didn't get a lot of aristocratic assistance. Irish King Fedelmid started robbing and wrecking more monks than the Vikings, but the monks fought back and killed him in 847. God must have finally decided to help Her disciples.

By 846 Malachy MacMulrooney emerged as a high king to rule all of the island, but it wasn't hereditary – unity came and went over the years. It was certainly 'went' when the Norman

'Strongbow' arrived in 1170 to take over Leinster, and Henry II rose to power in 1171. He was able to capitalize on Strongbow's foothold on the island and control most of the country with little resistance. Henry II told the Irish he had Pope Adrian IV's blessing. A Papal bull called *Laudabiliter* – issued back in 1155 – said the Irish should roll over and let Henry sort out their churches. (Some historians say the cunning king invented *Laudabiliter*, and it was a load of bull.)

Henry imposed his rule over Ireland by declaring his son, John, to be 'Lord of Ireland'. John then gave his consent to the Norman lords conquering more land. They built castles and towns, roads and bridges and instituted better agricultural practices. They also introduced English law, but could be brutal and oppressive in enforcing it. The medieval monarchs of England never conquered the whole island and the Irish persisted in rebelling – something that wouldn't change down the centuries. The Irish natives were exploited; something else that wouldn't change.

We have generally forgotten the Irish famine that happened five centuries before the notorious Famine of 1845, but it's a key moment in history. The rains of 1315 never stopped. They washed away the soils and flattened the crops and ruined the windmills that ground the grain. So hunger came upon the whole of Ireland. But the misery of that year was compounded by an invasion – not from the south of Britain but from Scotland. It was led by Edward Bruce, whose aim was to attack the English lords there. Any food left from the rains was destroyed by the Scots or stolen to feed their army. They say the armies of the English lords were eating Scottish prisoners while the peasants survived by eating dogs and horses.

It couldn't get much worse. But it did. In 1316 the year was just as cold, and the rain was just as heavy as the year before. The corn was just too wet to cut and hay for animals simply rotted in the fields. And still the Scots stravaiged around the countryside and stole what food there was. In 1317, winter cold arrived and froze the land. The peasants would have good harvests for the first time in three years, but the problem was hiding it from the starving Scottish soldiers. Then, in 1318, a chronicle reports: 'Edward Bruce who ruined the people of Ireland was by the people of Ireland killed near Dundalk after fierce fighting. And never was there a better deed done for the Irish than this since the beginning of time.'

Then came snow, the like of which had not been seen for many a year. It would come to be known as a Little Ice Age. Couldn't get worse? It did. After famine came a plague in 1322 and again in 1324. In 1327 came a deadly smallpox epidemic. In 1328 freak thunderstorms left much of the fruit and corn ruined and folk went hungry, suffering through terrible winds in the summer. In 1335 heavy snow in the spring killed most of the small birds in Ireland and three years later nearly all of the sheep died. At last, there were ten years of relative calm and the Irish must have thought their run of bad luck was over. They didn't see what was coming. By the end of the 1300s came the great mortality: Black Death.

In the 1400s the English were getting nervous about Irish resistance to rule from across the Irish Sea. They created a safe zone round Dublin, turning it into a sort of fortress called 'the Pale'. The Irish outside were said to be 'beyond the pale' – a phrase still enjoyed by speakers of the English language. King Richard II called those outside 'the wild Irish our enemies'. You could get thrown in jail in England just for being Irish. The English inside the Pale were urged to exterminate the 'wild Irish' outside 'like nettles'.

In 1485 the new Tudor family took over in England with Henry VII, who also hated Ireland. The Irish backed a rival pretender to the throne, Edward VI, and even had him 'crowned' in Dublin. 'Edward VI' was a fake and he failed in his invasion of England. Henry VII's son, Henry VIII, was too busy fighting foreign wars to complete the suppression of Irish unrest, but he did close the monasteries with his Reformation, the most provocative attack on the Catholic Irish peasants that could be imagined.

Elizabeth I inherited the unrest. Her majesty's governor in Ireland, the Earl of Sussex, said: 'I have often wished Ireland could be sunk in the sea.' No love lost there then. In 1569, when a rebellion broke out of the 'Wild Irish', the English commander murdered innocent farmers using the age-old reasoning: 'If they're dead they can't produce food to feed our enemies.'

In 1583 one of Elizabeth's lords, Sir Philip Sidney, visited Ulster. Sidney was a young soldier and poet who joined his father, Lord Deputy Henry Sidney, on a campaign to quell the Desmond Rebellion. While he was there he also took the opportunity to look at Irish culture. He spent the night in a peasant's home, where he experienced Irish poverty. He reported back: 'Half a dozen children, almost naked, were sleeping on a little straw with a pig, a dog, a cat, two chickens and a duck. The poor woman spread a mat on a chest, the only piece of furniture in the house and invited me to lie there. The animals greeted the first ray of the sun with their cries and began to look for something to eat ... I got up very soon for fear of being devoured.'

Sir Henry Sidney was less than sympathetic to the Irish rebels. His depredations were described by Sir Humphrey Gilbert, MP and soldier: Sidney ordered that the heads of all those rebels who were killed in one battle should be cut off. The heads were to be brought to his camp and laid on the ground by each side of the path leading into his tent. No one could come into his tent without passing through the lane of heads. Gilbert reported that this brought great terror to the people when they saw the heads of their dead fathers, brothers, children, relatives and friends lying on the ground before their faces.

Elizabeth's government came up with a solution to the Irish problem. Plantations. When rebel Irish lords lost their battles, their lands were handed over to English and Scottish Protestant settlers. Large areas of the Catholic north were given over to Protestant Scottish immigrants. The Plantation was intended to pacify Ulster, which had been an epicentre of rebellion for centuries. It was also intended to promote the spread of Protestantism in Ireland. The planters were required to build fortified houses and to clear the land for agriculture. They were also required to bring their families to Ireland and to raise their children as Protestants. By the end of the 1600s there were over a hundred thousand English and Scottish settlers in Ulster, and in the long term the impact of the Plantation of Ulster proved to be one of the most divisive policies in Britannia's history. As Liz may have said, 'It seemed like a good idea at the time.'

The good ideas don't end there. If Henry Sidney's cruelties

were bad, then Oliver Cromwell's attack on the country has been burnt into the Irish consciousness for almost four centuries. After the Parliamentarians had chopped Charles I they appointed Oliver Cromwell governor of Ireland – a job he clearly relished. He called Ireland 'That bleeding nation'.

A typical story (among hundreds) took place in Wexford, where two hundred women and children were herded into the marketplace to be slaughtered. Cromwell explained that this was a 'Righteous judgement' from God (I'm sure they all agreed). Priests in Wexford were flogged to death, then their bodies were flung into drains. Cromwell's soldiers would dress in Catholic priests' clothes to mock their victims, though it was said that they sickened and died soon after. A righteous judgement from God, eh Ollie? There were even stories that when they attacked a particularly well-defended place the English soldiers took Irish babies to use as shields.

English Catholics fought on the side of the Irish. Sir Arthur Aston, an English Catholic who led the defence of Drogheda north of Dublin, was captured. His wooden leg was ripped off and he was beaten to death with it. Cromwell's assassins believed it was full of gold – all they got were splinters.

Cromwell only stayed nine months; his legend has stayed for many generations. So did the enduring Irish Catholic opposition to English or British rule.

In the 1790s the Irish heard about the French Revolution and liked the idea. A man called Wolfe Tone founded 'the Society of United Irishmen' to start a rebellion. They were mostly Protestants who resented English control as much as the Catholics did.

The rebellion broke out in May 1798 and the rebels turned to France for help, but initially storms drove the French back (hints of the Armada there).

The plan was to attack Dublin under the cover of darkness. The street lamps were a problem. Tone's rebels came up with the ingenious idea of getting the lamplighters to go on strike. When they did, the British authorities sent soldiers with bayonets to prod the lamplighters back to work.

In August 1798 the French finally invaded – too late and too little, with just a thousand men, it was about as successful as the attempt to invade west Wales. Wolfe Tone was captured and sentenced to hang. On the morning of his execution he was found to have cut his windpipe with a penknife, but failed to cut the artery and was revived. The execution was put off. After a week in agony, a surgeon told Tone that if he tried to speak it would kill him. Tone replied: 'I can still find a word to thank you, sir. It is the most welcome news you could give me.' With that, he died.

That rebellion went on a little longer. Some United Irishmen started it up again in 1803, led by Robert Emmet – another Protestant. His rebellion was a miserable failure when only eighty men turned up with a single ladder to take Dublin Castle. Emmet was arrested and hanged. End of rebellion, but the relationship with Britain would only get worse.

The Great Famine of 1845 did nothing to endear the British to the Irish. Most farmers rented their land from absentee British landlords. And the British government was slow to respond to the suffering when the potato crops were destroyed by disease. When they did finally take action, it was often inadequate. Not only did they refuse to provide food aid to the Irish people, they were actually *exporting* food from Ireland during the famine. At least a million died and another two million emigrated.

When Irish farmers failed to pay their rents, their British landlords evicted them. The homeless families were driven into workhouses, where they suffered worse than hunger. A deadly typhus epidemic spread quickly through the malnourished population. A Doctor Stephens said: 'Then there was dysentery – known to the people as "Bloody Flux". The victims suffered agony from ulcers in the bowels. I could always tell if people in a cabin had Bloody Flux because the ground was covered with clots of blood. In Bantry workhouse I saw the living and the dead sharing a bed. There was no medicine, no water, no fire for warmth. The smell was like putting your head over a toilet pit.'

Some British landlords got rid of their peasants by paying their fares to the United States. But the journey could be a nightmare and many failed to make it. The ships became known as coffin ships; sixty sank before they even crossed the Atlantic.

Lord Lucan held sixty thousand acres. Suddenly short of staff, he decided to replace his Irish labourers with Scots. His argument against employing the Irish was: 'They are all Catholics. And I won't breed peasants to pay priests.' Religion was dividing the land yet again.

When the twentieth century arrived the Catholic Irish in the south were getting keen on 'Home Rule' to boot out the Brits while in Protestant Ulster in the north they began to organize themselves to *stop* Home Rule at any cost. The stage was set for a century of violence and misery (another one).

Ireland was offered Home Rule – but the onset of the First

World War delayed it. Not everyone could wait for the war to end. In 1916 an Easter Rising was led by the Irish Republican Brotherhood. They stood on the steps of Dublin Post Office and proclaimed Ireland free of the Brits. This simply got fifteen of them executed. Overreaction, as usual, only intensified the hatred of the ruling classes in Britain.

In 1919 came the Declaration of Independence, creating an Irish Free State in the south and Ulster in the north.* But the Catholics who lived as a minority in Ulster were treated as second-class citizens with fewer rights than the Protestants. In protest, the IRA launched a campaign of bombing and sabotage against Britain from January 1939 to March 1940. This campaign was known as the Sabotage Campaign or S-Plan. It was aimed at weakening Britain's infrastructure and forcing it to withdraw from Northern Ireland. The IRA carried out almost three hundred attacks and acts of sabotage in Britain, killing seven people and injuring 962.

Targets were mainly railways, government offices and power stations, in London, Birmingham, Manchester, Liverpool and Coventry. A bomb in the latter on 25 August 1939 claimed the lives of five civilians and was the campaign's deadliest incident. It was launched at a time when Britain was focused on the war with Germany, and the IRA hoped that the British resolve would be weakened. Of course it only served to harden that resolve. Two enemies, one determination: the Blitz Spirit, as it became known.

Worse was yet to come for Ireland. In 1968 came the start of

---

* This meant that while the whole island of Ireland was part of the British Isles, only Northern Ireland was part of the United Kingdom.

the so-called 'Troubles' between the IRA, which supported the Catholics who wanted to be part of the Republic of Ireland, and 'Loyalists' who fought for the Protestants and wanted to stay part of Britain. Violence grew as both sides started to use guns. Britain sent in soldiers to police the conflicts – theoretically pro-peace but pretty obviously pro-British – while the IRA and Loyalist armies grew stronger.

In 1971 the first British soldier was killed in Northern Ireland. Sadly, there would be another forty-one that year, and hundreds more in years to come as the Troubles got out of hand.

People from Northern Ireland were being imprisoned without trial. Over 90 per cent were Catholic, so on 30 January 1972 around fifteen thousand people gathered in the Bogside area of Derry to protest. What happened next has become known as 'Bloody Sunday'.

British soldiers were sent to police the crowds. They used rubber bullets and batons, then turned to using live ammunition. The army recorded that twenty-one soldiers fired 108 live rounds. Fourteen protestors died. All were Catholic. Yet an inquiry reported some of the soldiers' shooting as 'bordering on the reckless', but accepted their claims that they shot at gunmen and bomb-throwers. It later turned out that none of those attackers had weapons. 'Reckless' is an understatement.*

The massacre helped unite Irish Republican sentiments against

---

* A 1992 inquiry reversed the first inquiry's findings and later British Prime Minister David Cameron formally apologized. Cameron went on to become Lord Cameron of Chipping Norton. The Bloody Sunday victims did not.

Britain and its military. In 1973 IRA bombs were detonated in mainland Britain, then on 4 February 1974 came the notorious M62 coach bombing in which twelve died. The targets were the British military personnel and their families who were travelling on the coach.

A twenty-five-year-old woman with a personality disorder was convicted and served seventeen years in prison before it was revealed that the police had withheld evidence that would have exonerated her. Judith Ward had been hundreds of miles away in Chipping Norton at the time of the bombing, travelling with a circus. The real clowns were the police. The investigation that generated evidence to convict Judith Ward was led by Detective Chief Superintendent George Oldfield. (This is the man who also failed to cover himself with glory as the investigator of the Yorkshire Ripper case in the years that followed. A policeman's lot is not a happy one.) The massive miscarriage of justice did nothing for Anglo–Irish relationships when Judith Ward's conviction was overturned in 1992.

Even in the misery of the Troubles, typical Irish black humour survived. In 1976, slogans on Belfast walls included 'No pope here' – underneath it someone wrote, 'Lucky old pope'. Eventually the violence defeated its own object as the deaths of innocents became sickening. The tide began to turn against the violence. The conflict was formally ended with the Belfast or Good Friday Agreement of 1998. In August that year, a protest bombing in Omagh killed twenty-nine innocent people, but if anything it served to strengthen the argument for peace.

Like many of those Britain has fought with, Ireland has played a key role in Britain's own history. But despite Ireland having been a member of the United Kingdom, for hundreds of years one of the most important parts of being in the English ruling classes was being non-Irish and non-Catholic. Could it be said that violence in Ireland ever united the people of Britain? Perhaps in the past. But as religious zeal has diminished, so have the hatreds. The passionate Protestant priest Ian Paisley said in 1997, 'I will never sit down with [Catholic Irish leader] Gerry Adams . . . he'd sit with anyone. He'd sit down with the devil. In fact, Adams does sit down with the devil.' In March 2007 they not only met but shook hands and announced that they would form a power-sharing government in Northern Ireland.

Hatreds can unite people against a common enemy. But even the oldest hatreds can end in time. Maybe two thousand years of Irish suffering tips the balance in favour of peace.

10

GERMANY

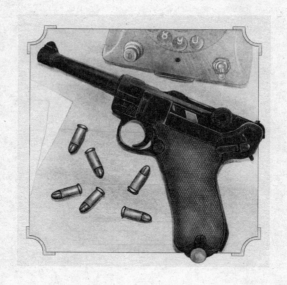

Be honest: when I said 'Britain's enemy', who did you think of?

The modern German state was founded long after the Angles and Saxons made their home in Britannia, in January 1871, when the king of Prussia, Wilhelm I, was proclaimed German Emperor in the Hall of Mirrors at the Palace of Versailles in France. It's often said that this event marked the end of the Franco–Prussian War and the unification of Germany into a single 'nation-state', but if Will the First was an 'emperor', then the new nation already saw itself as an empire. Ambitious to expand from the moment of birth. Probably nothing to worry about.

Up to 1871, Germany was a collection of independent states, principalities and free cities. These were loosely united as a German Confederation, but each had its own government and laws. As well as being a loose political unity, they were united by a common culture and language. Above all they were united by a common enemy: France. Even more than Britannia, the German sheep flocked together to defend themselves against the *loup* across the border.

The Franco–Prussian War (which Germany won) defined the new nation as militaristic. In time its people would be stereotyped by their sausages, beer, lederhosen and efficiency. If the French ate frogs and became 'Frogs', then the Germans ate fermented cabbage called sauerkraut and were dubbed 'Krauts' by American soldiers in the First World War. The alleged German lack of humour could have labelled them Sour Krauts. This is extremely unfair. Even in its short history, Germany has given the world some great gifts. Reliable motor cars for one thing . . . and garden gnomes for twenty-five million other things. (They were first made in Thuringia 120 years ago.)

Karl Benz (1844–1929) may have invented the first practical automobile powered by an internal combustion engine in 1885, a three-wheeled vehicle with a four-stroke engine that could reach speeds of up to sixteen km/h (ten mph). But he never drove it more than a few miles. His wife, Bertha (1849–1944), was braver. In 1888 she decided to take her two sons from their house in Mannheim to her home town in Pforzheim, a daunting 105 kilometres. She told no one – not even her husband Karl – where they were going.

As they puttered along, Bertha told the boys how she had helped Karl to design the car. The leather brake linings? Her idea. The fuel system? Her idea. But because she was a woman, she couldn't have her name on her inventions under German law. Karl Benz would become rich and famous, but he owed it all to Bertha. In 1900 a businessman in Germany, Emil Jellinek, put money into the Daimler car company and their cars were named after his daughter, Mercedes. When the company joined with Benz the Mercedes-Benz was born. But in a fairer world, people would be driving a Bertha.

Every silver lining has a cloud and the German genius for

technology was grasped by the militaristic minds of the new nation. Benz engines were used to power weapons of mass destruction like Zeppelin airship bombers and fighter aeroplanes. The united Germany had found a new opponent to unite against. It was Britain. And, oddly, conflicts with Germany – the First and Second World Wars – would serve to unite Britain in a way no enemy ever had before.

Ironically, Germans had been ruling Britain for two hundred years before the First World War threatened a German invasion.

The history of Britain being ruled by families from outside England is a long one. After the Normans became anglicized, the Tudors from Wales took over in 1485 and annexed Wales to England. After Elizabeth I's death in 1603, the Scottish Stuarts ruled for another hundred years. King James brought the north Britons and the south Britons together with a flag, the Union Jack. It was a combination of the flags of England (the red cross of St George) and Scotland (the white saltire of St Andrew). (The presence of Wales was just implied.) The Union Jack was originally used for maritime purposes only, but it gradually became the national flag of Great Britain and later the United Kingdom. In 1707 the Act of Union finally united the Scots in the north with the Welsh and English in the south. It was an arranged marriage – arranged by the politicians, but not necessarily by the people. Ireland was not represented on the flag until the Act of Union of 1800 merged the Kingdom of Great Britain and the Kingdom of Ireland to form the United Kingdom of Great Britain and Ireland. The new design added a red saltire, the cross of St Patrick, for Ireland.

The Act of Union was the first union of the countries of the British Isles coming under one rule based in London. Up to that time, there had been over a thousand years of foreign rulers. Then, more than a millennium after they first arrived, the Germans made an unexpected comeback as rulers of Britannia. They would stay. And stay. It doesn't look as though they will be going anywhere soon.

Queen Anne (1665–1714) had been the last of the Stuarts. She took the throne in 1702, but was the only monarch ever to have been carried to their coronation. The new queen was too fond of her food, and she had developed gout so badly that her legs wouldn't support her.

She and husband George had tried for an heir. They really tried: Anne became pregnant eighteen times, but seventeen babies died before or soon after birth. Only little William survived a while. But when weak Will reached the age of eleven he must have realized he was a bit odd, living so long. So he popped his clogs.

Clearly Anne and George were enthusiastic in the heir-making department, but not everyone was so enamoured of the queen's husband, Prince George of Denmark. George, they said, was no Viking. He was boring. Very boring. He suffered from asthma and when he had an attack he breathed very heavily (someone cruelly suggested that he did this to prove that he was still alive).

Anne was the first monarch to see a single Parliament for a United Kingdom. When the queen wasn't riding she took to attending the House of Lords in person. She sat on the throne and listened to the debates – or in winter sat on a bench by the fire. When she died, her doctor said: 'I believe sleep was never more welcome to a weary traveller than death was to her.' Goodnight to the last Stuart.*

Anne was shy, stout and short-sighted. Perhaps she did welcome death. Her coffin was almost square. If the House of Lords was the best 'entertainment' she could find it's no wonder she invented Royal Ascot.

Anne's lack of heirs was tragic for her and disastrous for Britain. It opened the door for a German royal family on the throne. The Saxon-Germans were back, and the new Hengist was George I from Hanover.

The German Georgians had their feet under the top table and Britain was slowly becoming a unit. That's not to say there was peace. The Scottish Catholics wanted the Stuarts back on the throne and rebelled. The Jacobite risings ended disastrously at the Battle of Culloden in 1746.

As we've seen, the American colonists rebelled, and Britain gained its independence from them. Unfettered by British law, the slave trade had been booming in the American colonies. Nicholas Cresswell, a visitor to the West Indies in 1774, said: 'We went ashore and saw a cargo of slaves land. They were all naked except for a small piece of blue cloth. If they made the slightest mistake they were tied up and whipped without mercy. Some of them die under this harsh treatment.'

---

* Some couldn't believe the news. When the chaplain of St John's College, Oxford expressed his doubts, the head of the college famously replied: 'She's as dead as Julius Caesar.'

In Britain pirates thrived, and highwaymen were heroes. Smuggling became a major industry, with half the population involved in some way. But it was a violent business. In 1748, for example, a man called Chater betrayed a smuggling gang and a law officer called Galley tried to arrest them. A publication of the time described what happened next:

> They began with poor Galley, cut off his nose, broke every joint of him and after several hours of torture dispatched him. Chater they carried to a dry well, hung him by the middle to a cross beam in it, leaving him to perish with hunger and pain. But when they came, several days after, and heard him groan, they cut the rope, let him drop to the bottom and threw in logs and stones to cover him. The person who told the magistrates the story was in disguise because he feared the same would happen to him.

Under the German Georgians the poor were poorer than ever. A mother and two children in Cumberland had no bread and tried to survive on horse bran. They were all found dead one morning and the children had straw in their mouths. The poverty drove others to suicide. The *Western Flying Post* newspaper reported in 1755: 'On 6th June an old man hanged himself by his handkerchief at Linkinhorne in Cornwall. The coroner decided that he had committed suicide. He was buried at Kesbrook Cross-road and a stake driven through his body.'

The desperate found inventive ways to make money. Body-snatching became a new sideline for the not-so-squeamish to keep surgeons supplied with corpses. Underground women's fighting was a sport enjoyed by thousands (along with bear-baiting, cock-fighting and dogs killing rats in pits). The winner would make a bit of money, but the loser got only a few coins thrown to her.

Meanwhile, the rich lived lavishly. Of course, they relied on some of the middle-class voters to keep them in power, but they rather resented the token 'democracy' they had to endure. Men (never women) who had a certain amount of land or property above a certain value could vote. Not all those who qualified met the social standards of the parliamentary candidates. Irish landowner John Boyle, 5th Earl of Cork (1707–62) spat: 'At election time I have to open my doors to every dirty fellow in the county who has a vote. All my best floors are spoiled by the hobnailed boots of the farmers stamping about them. Every room is a pigsty and the Chinese wallpaper in the drawing room stinks so terrible of tobacco that it would knock you down to walk into it.'

Queen Victoria came to the throne in 1837. Although history books prefer to see her reign as a new era, she was still a Saxe-Coburg-Gotha. Imagine the chagrin of her German relatives, then, when Britain went to war with Germany in 1914. The leader of the German enemy was Queen Victoria's grandson, Kaiser Wilhelm II. How embarrassing.

Queen Victoria had been very fond of little Wilhelm, and she hoped that he would become a close friend and ally of Britain. But Wilhelm II was ambitious, and he had his own ideas about Germany's role in the world. Wilhelm II's relationship with Britain deteriorated over time. He was jealous of Britain's global power, and he resented Britain's attempts to contain Germany's growth.

Wilhelm II was determined to test Germany's strength against Britain, and he believed that Germany could win a quick and decisive victory. But little Willy underestimated Britain's resolve. He prompted Scotland, Wales and England to pull together and become a truly United Kingdom in the face of German hostility. (Ireland, as we've seen, was a different matter.) And so the family of Wilhelm's nan decided it was time to drop the German family name of Saxe-Coburg-Gotha, opting instead for the hearty name of their favourite Berkshire castle, Windsor.

The First World War had deep roots. On 18 January 1871, when the German princes gathered at Versailles and proclaimed the Prussian King Wilhelm I – Queen Victoria's son-in-law – the German Emperor, his chancellor, Otto von Bismarck, the unifier, came up with a far-reaching policy. Millions of non-German subjects living in the new German Empire – the Polish, Danish and French minorities – were discriminated against. From there, a policy of 'Germanization' evolved.

The new empire was authoritarian, and the constitution gave the emperor power to appoint or dismiss the chancellor. He was supreme commander-in-chief of the armed forces and decided foreign policy. That's fine if the emperor is a sensible person. It can be disastrous when he is unpredictable and paranoid, like Wilhelm II.

Wilhelm I had died in 1888 and his son Frederick – Fritz to his friends – took over. He failed to score a century when he died after ruling for just ninety-nine days. He was fifty-six. It was one of those premature deaths that many historians say changed the course of German and European history. Fritz did not agree with

Bismarck or his plans for German military expansion. And, when the court priest campaigned to persecute Germany's Jews, Fritz opposed it. He was backed by his wife, Princess Victoria (1840–1901) – eldest daughter of Queen Victoria across the Channel – who said: 'The German enemies of the Jews behave so hatefully towards people of a different faith, and another race, who become an integral part – and by no means the worst – of our nation.'

Germany under Fritz and Empress Victoria could have been so different. But Fritz had a weakness for cigarettes, and it killed him. Cancer of the larynx. As the Irish playwright George Bernard Shaw (1856–1950) said: 'A cigarette is a pinch of tobacco rolled in paper with fire at one end and a fool at the other.' In the history books of the world, the cigarette and its depredations have been ignored, yet it killed every British monarch who died in the twentieth century.

Fritz's son Wilhelm II took the reins in 1888 as the third German ruler of that year. He once said: 'Give me a woman who loves beer, and I will conquer the world.' This doesn't sound like the sort of man that will make his enemies quake in their marching boots, but he had militaristic tendencies. Little Willy was never popular. His grandmother, Queen Victoria of Britain, came to despair of him. His (British) mother, Empress Victoria, refused to wish him a happy birthday when his views conflicted with her own liberal opinions ... so he sulked for days. His father, Fritz, had always said he would be a dangerous leader (smart Dad). As soon as Fritz died, William II ordered the occupation of the imperial residence by soldiers. The rooms of Fritz and Victoria were searched for his mother's letters that may have reflected badly on the new kaiser. They did exist – but wise Mum had sent them all to Windsor Castle the previous year.

Wilhelm II had been born with a withered left arm and it embarrassed him. When he was photographed he insisted on hiding his weak arm. People around him hid their left arms too. Wilhelm was so insecure he felt driven to demonstrate his power. So when German workers went on strike, he ordered soldiers to attack the strikers. He said, 'I expect my troops to shoot at least five hundred.'

France and Britannia were the enemy in Wilhelm's twisted vision. Their best response was predictable: stand shoulder to shoulder against this upstart aggressor. The French and British marked the end of almost a thousand years of belligerence with a treaty known as the Entente Cordiale in 1904. Wilhelm and Germany retaliated by making alliances of their own. War was becoming inevitable. Everyone saw that. What they didn't see – couldn't see – were the killing fields, the endless graveyards. They probably didn't predict that the first shot would be fired by the most obscure ally of all, Serbia.

Why did the so-called Great War start? Lots of big, thick history books have been written to answer that question. But, to put it simply, by 1914 the countries of Europe had formed into two big gangs. The gang called the 'Central Powers' were led by the Germans and the 'Allies' were led by the French and British. The two gangs started collecting weapons, making threats and swapping insults, the way gangs do. All it needed was for one gang member to throw the first stone and a huge punch-up would follow.

It began when a Serbian gang known as the Black Hand (honest) waited till the Austrian emperor came to Bosnia. Serbia (Allies) was struggling to free itself from the rule of Austria-Hungary (Central Powers) and a Serbian expressed his protest by shooting the heir to the Austro-Hungarian throne. The assassination of Archduke Ferdinand that started the First World War was a cack-handed affair and he was shot despite the Black Hand bunglers' worst efforts. Ferdi was due to drive through Sarajevo, so the Black Hand armed themselves with guns and bombs at different parts of the route. There were seven assassins in the plot to kill the archduke, heir to the Austrian Empire.

Assassin #1 failed. The procession passed. He did nothing. Then Assassin #2, Čabrinović, nearly succeeded. He threw his bomb into Ferdi's car. Ferdi picked it up and threw it out of the car. The bomb blew up under the following car and injured eight innocent people. Number 2 swallowed poison and jumped in the river to drown rather than be captured. But the crowd dragged him out, saved him and then nearly beat him to death.

Ferdi drove on to the town hall and made a speech. He was in reach of would-be-assassins 3, 4, 5 and 6. And they, erm, did nothing. Next, Ferdi headed for the hospital to visit the bomb victims. By an amazing coincidence, his driver took a wrong turning. Slightly off-route, they drove straight past Assassin #7, Gavrilo Princip. Princip jumped on to the open car and fired two shots, killing Ferdi and his wife.

Ferdi's dad, the emperor of Austria, was furious. He wanted revenge; he wanted war. The first stone had been thrown. Austria declared war on Serbia; Germany helped Austria; so Russia helped Serbia; so France helped Russia. Germany marched through Belgium to get to France; so Britain helped Belgium.

The Great War had started. It was expected to last about four months. It lasted four years.

The mood of defiance created the British 'characteristic' of keeping a 'stiff upper lip' in the face of suffering. The other characteristic was the 'sporting' metaphor that unchivalrous conduct was 'just not cricket'. Where did this illusion of fair play as a British character ideal come from?

Maybe from a poem. A poem that changed the world, some believe. Henry Newbolt (1862–1938) was an English writer whose reputation was established in 1897 with a poem written about a schoolboy cricketer who grew up to fight in the Boer Wars, 'Vitai Lampada'. In the panic of battle the boy is stirred to heroic action by schooldays memories: 'his Captain's hand on his shoulder smote – Play up! play up! and play the game!'.

Translating the spirit of cricket on to the battlefield became an image of martyrdom for king and country. The second verse saw the schoolboy years later.

> The sand of the desert is sodden red, –
> Red with the wreck of a square that broke; –
> The Gatling's jammed and the colonel dead,
> And the regiment blind with dust and smoke.
> The river of death has brimmed his banks,
> And England's far, and Honour a name,
> But the voice of a schoolboy rallies the ranks:
> 'Play up! play up! and play the game!'

Those famous words expressed the view, more common at the time, that war should be fought in the same spirit as school sports, and the poem was publicly acclaimed at the time of its publication. But, as the terror of the trenches set in, it lost out to the cynical poets who saw that war was no game and patriotism was an illusion – the most famous of these, taught in schools more than a century later, is Wilfred Owen (1893–1918).

Newbolt would have agreed with Owen by the end of the First World War. He came to dislike his most famous poem. He was constantly called upon to recite it and by 1923 sighed: 'It's a kind of Frankenstein's Monster that I created thirty years ago.'

Henry Tandey (1891–1977) played the game. He won a VC for his actions in France during the First World War. The citation of 14 December 1918 read:

> For most conspicuous bravery and initiative during the capture of the village and the crossings at Marcoing when, during the advance, his platoon was held up by machine-gun fire. He at once crawled forward, located the machine gun, and, with a Lewis gun team, knocked it out. Later in the evening, during an attack, he, with eight comrades, led a bayonet charge, fighting so fiercely that 37 of the enemy were driven into the hands of the remainder of his company. Although twice wounded, he refused to leave till the fight was won.

Tandey was an exceptionally brave man. He'd fought and survived some of the war's greatest battles; he was at the First Battle of Ypres in October 1914, and two years later he was wounded in the leg during the Battle of the Somme, then wounded at Passchendaele in November 1917. Then he arrived at Marcoing on that VC action.

But what happened earlier that day was more sensational. Tandey was told to attack a German trench and – informally – to take no prisoners. Prisoners have to be escorted back to the British lines and that takes a valuable British fighting man out of action.

As the brutal battle reached its climax, the enemy troops surrendered or retreated. A wounded German soldier limped out of the trench and into Private Tandey's line of fire. The exhausted German soldier didn't even raise his rifle. He simply stared at Tandey and waited to be shot. That's when Tandey's sporting 'Vitaï Lampada' instinct kicked in. Shoot a helpless man? Not cricket, old boy. Henry Tandey in his own words later stated: 'I took aim but couldn't shoot a wounded man, so I let him go.'*

The young German soldier nodded a silent *Danke* and retreated to safety as fast as his twenty-nine-year-old legs would carry him. The lucky German ended up back in Germany, where he languished in the humiliation of defeat. He began to campaign for a resurgence in German power. Revenge, in fact. He had a passionate hatred of the 'traitors' in Germany who had cost them the war. He especially blamed Jewish people for supposedly being responsible for Germany's surrender. He later said: 'We are going to destroy the Jews. They are not going to get away with what they did on 9 November 1918. The day of reckoning has come.'

---

* The notoriously unsporting cricketer W. G. Grace would not have approved. For once W. G. would have been right.

When he saw a newspaper cutting showing Tandey being awarded the Victoria Cross, he said: 'That man came so near to killing me that I thought I should never see Germany again. Providence saved me from such devilishly accurate fire as those English boys were aiming at us.'

The name of the German was, you'll have guessed, Adolf Hitler. The bullet that Gavrilo Princip fired to start the First World War led to millions of deaths. The bullet Tandey didn't fire at Hitler caused countless millions more.

When Tandey was told much later what he had done in a moment of British fair play he said he regretted it. 'I'd give ten years now to have five minutes of clairvoyance then.' But Tandey played by the rules: you never argue with the umpire's decision. And you don't shoot a man when he's down. Play up and play the game.

There were lots of tragedies in the Great War. Almost every family in Britain, France, Germany and Russia lost someone. You can go to any town or village and see the lists of the dead, carved in stone memorials. Many of the men who joined together died together and left their home towns desolate.

But that wasn't the real tragedy. The cruellest thing of all was that the First World War didn't solve any problems and it didn't bring peace. It led to the Second World War and far, far more misery, death and destruction. Those whose names are carved on the memorials believed they were fighting for peace. Many gave their lives with the consolation of knowing they had died in 'the war to end all wars'. What went wrong?

Britain and France celebrated their new-found friendship.

Germany seethed at her unbearable defeat. In fact, many Germans refused to accept that they were defeated. The Armistice on 11 November 1918 had stopped the war on the German borders – the Allies had never set foot on German soil. Agitators said it wasn't a defeat; it was traitors within Germany who had called a temporary halt to hostilities. That was nonsense, but as a famous German once said: 'If you tell a lie big enough and keep repeating it, people will eventually come to believe it.'*

Britannia had been united by defiance in the First World War, as well as in mourning for many more who died of the Spanish Flu epidemic that followed. If Wilhelm II was spoiling for the fight that led to the First World War, then it seemed as if Hitler's Germany was not out for revenge against Britannia. Hitler especially hated the Communist Russian regime (which, strangely, he thought was somehow also Jewish), but had a respect for the British. He didn't understand why the British and French didn't see the bleedin' obvious. The dictator said: 'Everything I undertake is directed against Russia. If the West is too stupid and blind to grasp this, then I shall be compelled to come to an agreement with Russia, beat the West and then after their defeat turn against the Soviet Union with all my forces.'

In turn the British were slow to condemn him. In fact, in their British way, they found something to admire in the megalomaniac: his patriotism. A British politician called Winston Churchill wrote an article in *The Strand* magazine in 1935: 'One

---

* That eloquent German was apparently the Nazi propagandist Joseph Goebbels. It might not have been him, but it has been repeated so often that people believe it.

may dislike Hitler's system and yet admire his patriotic achievement. If our country were defeated, I hope we should find a champion as indomitable to restore our courage and lead us back to our place among the nations.' High praise indeed.

Some people argue that Hitler's desire to commit genocide only became clear when it was too late. Yet his rage against the Jewish people was quite open. As early as 1922 he had ranted:

> Once I really am in power, my first and foremost task will be the annihilation of the Jews. As soon as I have the power to do so, I will have gallows built in rows – at the Marienplatz in Munich, for example – as many as traffic allows. Then the Jews will be hanged indiscriminately, and they will remain hanging until they stink; they will hang there as long as the principles of hygiene permit. As soon as they have been untied, the next batch will be strung up, and so on down the line, until the last Jew in Munich has been exterminated. Other cities will follow suit, precisely in this fashion, until all Germany has been completely cleansed of Jews.

So maybe there was a bit of a clue there that we were dealing with a fanatic and nothing good would come of it. But the Allies – the 'winners' of the First World War – stood by and watched this psychopath Blitz his way to power and turn Germany into a fortress.

Hitler made alliances with Franco's Spain and Mussolini's Italy and demanded that Czechoslovakia hand over parts of its country populated by Germans – they came up with the name Sudetenland for the region. Hitler said Germany should invade and occupy the Sudetenland to show the world he meant business. British Prime Minister Neville Chamberlain did not show the bulldog spirit Britain was famed for. He met Hitler in Munich in 1938 and came home waving a piece of paper and declaiming, 'Peace for our time.' It wasn't even peace for a Munich-born baby to see its first birthday. Hitler wanted German Czechoslovakia? Oh, go on then, Adolf old chap, you take it. 'Appeasement' was the word attached to the un-British climbdown.

Winston '[I] admire Hitler's patriotic achievement' Churchill expressed the mood of the backlash: 'England has been offered a choice between war and shame. She has chosen shame and will get war.'

Hitler 'got away with' Sudetenland. He pushed his luck by invading the whole of Czechoslovakia. Enough's enough. Well, almost enough. The British drew a line in the sand: invade Poland and we will fight you. Hitler invaded anyway.

Britain was at war. In the 1930s Mr Hitler and his German forces had come up with the idea of 'Blitzkrieg' or 'Lightning War'. General Guderian told the German Army how to beat Poland: hit it with thousands of bombs from the air and smash its defences. Then send in tanks. Knock the Poles out before they know what has hit them.

Some Brits appeared blasé at the prospect of a bombing campaign against cities. John Betjeman was a poet who went on to be Poet Laureate. He wrote a poem, 'Slough', which may have been funny in 1937:

Come, friendly bombs, and fall on Slough!
It isn't fit for humans now

By 1940 it looked tasteless. The Blitz was to have been the precursor of an invasion. Operation Sea Lion (or *Unternehmen Seelöwe*, as they say in Berlin) was Hitler's code name for the plan for an invasion of Britain. Back in 1939 France had fallen in six weeks and the Führer was sure the British government would sue for peace. Sea Lion was to be a last resort. An invasion would need both air and naval superiority over the English Channel and the proposed landing sites. A large number of barges were gathered together on the defeated French coast, but that air superiority was as elusive as a vegan in an abattoir.

Blitzkrieg may have worked in Poland, but Britain had a well-organized air defence system – the Royal Air Force – and it was about to be called upon as never before (or since). Winston Churchill had taken over as British war leader on 10 May 1940, when he was appointed prime minister following the resignation of Neville Chamberlain. In a speech to the House of Commons on 20 August 1940 he thanked the RAF for winning the aerial battle against all odds. He came up with one of his many quotes that would epitomize British heroism: 'Never in the field of human conflict was so much owed by so many to so few.'

When those plans to bomb RAF aerodromes failed, the German bombers started to target London's docks on the Thames to wreck Britain's supplies and fighting ships. But on 24 August 1940, German night bombers drifted off course and accidentally destroyed several London homes. It was a blunder. Churchill ordered the RAF to make a revenge attack on Berlin the next night. In response, Hitler raged: 'And should the Royal Air Force drop two thousand, or three thousand kilograms then we will now drop one million kilograms in a single night. And should they increase their attacks on our cities, then we will erase their cities.' The tiger had been prodded with a sharp stick.

September 15 has become 'Battle of Britain Day'. On that day in 1940, the Luftwaffe assembled their largest bombing attack yet. The entire RAF was called to the defence of London and the South East. The outcome was a decisive British victory that proved to mark a turning point in the invasion. Two days later, Hitler postponed Sea Lion indefinitely. Thank you, RAF.

Still, Hitler intended to keep his promise to 'erase' Britain's cities. The Blitz had begun. Over the next five years bombs and rockets fell nightly on Britain. But far from breaking British morale it generated a spirit of defiant togetherness that has become legendary: Blitz Spirit.

Herbert Morrison (1888–1965), the wartime home secretary, designed a domestic bomb shelter for any home with a patch of garden. He tested it. Did he drop a bomb on it? No, this is Britain, remember. He had one erected then jumped up and down on the roof. The British responded with characteristic eccentricity. They bought tickets for the Underground and went down to shelter there 'legally'.

Another aspect of the British character had been the class system. It was about to be tested with another government policy – evacuation of children from the cities to the countryside to save them from the bombing. It brought home the class divides when city children were billeted with the genteel folk of the country. Their habits were at variance. One city woman reportedly took her child to his new billet in the country. She was shocked when her six-year-old dropped his trousers and started to poo in the middle of the living room. His mother screamed at him: 'You dirty thing, messing up the lady's carpet. Do what we taught you at home. Go and do it in the corner.'

Stories of blissful billeting in the country abound. The failures are forgotten. Failures like the children who said: 'I was so miserable I tried to cut my own throat . . . but the knife was blunt,' or 'I was beaten at least once a week with a stick, a poker, a wooden spoon – anything that was handy. I wanted to drown myself in the ditch behind the house.' Other children complained: 'The billetors stole everything we had – toys and the clothes that fitted their own children.' They were encouraged to lie about their experience. A child remembered: 'My sister Anne started to lose her hair and we were getting scabs on our heads and bodies, but they told us to write good things in our letters home.' Another recalled, 'I was always hungry and had a bad case of worms in my stomach, but I didn't dare tell anyone.'

Worms or bombs? The Blitz began with fifty-seven nights of consecutive raids on London, although one of the most devastating raids was on Coventry on 14 November 1940. By the time the Blitz ended in May 1941 some forty-three thousand civilians had been killed, half of them in London.

After the war, the myth of the plucky Blitz Spirit only grew, as reflected in the TV series *Dad's Army*:

'There's a war on, Dad.'
'Oh, I wondered what the noise was.'

This idea of defiance and endurance goes to the heart of what many regard as 'Britishness'. The iconic year 1940 held the triptych of Britain's war memory: Dunkirk, the Battle of Britain and the Blitz. The Blitz Spirit is rooted deep in the British collective memory. But did it exist in the 1940s?

There are many tales of Blitz Spirit. One touching one comes from Cardiff, identified by Hitler as a 'vital harbour installation'. On 2 January 1941 more than a hundred Luftwaffe planes dropped high-explosive bombs and fourteen thousand incendiaries on the city. Over sixty people were killed in one suburb in the first half-hour of the raid. In one of the streets, a rescue party dug for several hours to free a six-year-old child trapped under a staircase. As they dug, the boy sang 'God Save The King' repeatedly. He was rescued and explained the singing. He said his father, a coal miner, had told him that when men were trapped underground they kept on singing to keep their spirits up. The national anthem was the only song for which he knew the words. Now that's what I call Blitz Spirit.

Other stories show that this spirit was not universal. While the poor huddled in their tinny Anderson shelters, the rich stayed comfortable even in the cities. At the Dorchester Hotel the management converted the cellars into posh shelters for those who could afford it. Nine peers slept there most nights. They included Lord Halifax, the foreign secretary, waited on by hotel staff and sustained with a supply of his favourite whisky.

Some people exploited the Blitz for their own gain. 'Bomb-chasers' followed the raids so they could loot shops or houses while the occupants were in the shelters. Far from sharing amid the suffering, a black market in stolen goods and ration coupons thrived. The 'spivs' who were the face of shady deals became a national obsession. In London some seeking shelter were charged money to get a place on the Tube to sleep at night. At the cinema, many bomb victims were angry to discover that the newsreel was all about the destruction of Coventry; Hull had suffered the loss of 85 per cent of its buildings but was only referred to as 'a North East town'.

Mass-observation investigators, whose job was to monitor levels of public morale, reported on the Coventry Blitz:

> There was an unprecedented dislocation and depression in Coventry the next day. There were more open signs of hysteria, terror and neurosis observed in one evening than during the whole of the past two months together in all areas. People were seen to cry, to scream, to tremble all over, to faint in the street, to attack a fireman. The overwhelmingly dominant feeling was one of utter helplessness. The tremendous impact of the previous night had left people practically speechless.

Crime flourished. In February 1942 Evelyn Hamilton, a forty-year-old chemist, headed out into the blackout for supper at a Lyons Corner House. She would not return to her boarding house. The next morning – Monday, 9 February 1942 – two men on their way to work spotted a torch lying on the ground near an air raid shelter. When they looked inside they found Evelyn Hamilton; she had been strangled.

The next day, two meter readers entered a flat in Soho and their torches picked out the body of a woman with her head hanging over the edge of the bed. She was Evelyn Oatley, thirty-five; she'd been strangled and her throat had been cut. She had also been mutilated using a torch, a razor blade, a tin opener and hair tongs. Chief Superintendent Fred Cherrill of Scotland Yard declared: 'Not since the panic-ridden days in 1888, when Jack the Ripper was abroad in the East End, had London known such a reign of terror.'

This serial killer was undone by the number on his gas-mask case, which he dropped. That led the police to his room, where they found him wearing a bloodstained shirt and with items he'd stolen from his victims. The trial was brief, and within thirty-five minutes the jury found him guilty. He was executed on 25 June 1942 at Wandsworth Prison. The punishment fitted the crime: he was hanged during an air raid.

Whether or not the Blitz Spirit defined the experience of the war, there is little doubt that the intensity of the fighting at home and abroad helped shape Britain's national identity. The British still believe that they are best when their backs are against the wall – when they stand alone. (Except in penalty shootouts.) That was reflected in the 2016 referendum, when British voters were asked if they wanted to be part of Europe and – to the surprise of the governing establishment – they said 'No'.

Geoffrey Wellum (1921–2018) was the youngest Spitfire pilot in the Battle of Britain. He may have been speaking for the Brexit voters when he said the Germans were not perceived as the real enemy. He said: 'The enemy were always respected. Real hatred is reserved for the politicians who send men to war. I realize how bloody stupid they are.'

Hatred of Germany and the Germans faded, sometimes slowly and sometimes with an unexpected leap. People like Bert Trautmann made even the diehard Brit nationalists realize that

German people could be goodies too. If you don't know his story, then it is simply told – though the impact on the British public was greater at the time than you'd imagine.

Bert Trautmann (1923–2013) was a German professional footballer who served as a paratrooper in the Second World War. He was one of just ninety from his regiment of a thousand who survived, captured in 1944 and held as a prisoner of war in Lancashire. When the war ended, he declined to be repatriated and took a job as a farm worker, playing part-time as a goalkeeper for the local football team. Bert turned out to be so good he was signed to play professionally for Manchester City.

He played as a goalkeeper for Manchester City from 1949 to 1964. So far, so ordinary. But the defining moment of his life came in the 1956 FA Cup Final. With seventeen minutes of the match to go, Trautmann suffered a serious injury while diving at the feet of Birmingham City's Peter Murphy. There were no substitutes in those days, so the dazed Trautmann carried on. He made vital saves to hold on to his team's 3–1 lead and collected his winner's medal. Trautmann later said, 'I played in a kind of a fog.'

The first hospital sent him home, telling him he had a crick in the neck. Three days later an X-ray revealed he had dislocated five vertebrae in his neck, the second of which was cracked in two. The third vertebra had wedged against the second, preventing further damage which could have cost Trautmann his life. That's some crick in the neck.

It was the sort of story that even the writers of *Roy of the Rovers* couldn't make up. A small accident but a massive impact on the British view of German people. A German had lived the 'Vitai Lampada' ideal: 'Play up and play the game – even if your neck is broken.' And children stopped playing German baddies. Bob Wilson (b. 1941), the former Arsenal and Scotland goalkeeper, expressed it concisely when he said Bert was an 'amazing man who helped bring our warring countries closer together'.

Yet there are still Britons who 'remember' the miseries inflicted by the Second World War and refuse to forgive Germans. Beneath one 2018 article in the *Daily Express* about the Blitz, a Brexiteer reader responded: 'Remainer kids take note, this is what Germany is capable of and though the bombs and planes have disappeared, they still use threats and economical warfare through the EU to dominate Europe.' The patriots are on the move. If they learnt how to write correct English they'd be dangerous.

As Johnson (Samuel, not Boris) famously said: 'Patriotism is the last refuge of a scoundrel.' Now we know patriotism is also the last refuge of the village idiot.

From Saxons to Nazis, for better and worse, the Germanic people have helped shape Britannia. In the wars of the twentieth century, as in all wars, there was monumental suffering, and after two world wars people generally agreed that it should never happen again.

EPILOGUE

> *'The British are special. The world knows it.
> In our innermost thoughts we know it.
> This is the greatest nation on Earth.'*

Perhaps now we are ready to answer the question of how some Britons came to believe that their *other* Eden is superior.

Take delusional verse like that of William Blake (1757–1827):

And did those feet in ancient time
Walk upon England's mountains green:
And was the holy Lamb of God,
On England's pleasant pastures seen?

Erm ... no, Jesus certainly didn't walk upon England's mountains green. Don't be silly, Willie. And if there is to be a second coming, it won't be in Britain, mate. He wouldn't be allowed to disembark at Dover because he was an immigrant with no passport. Asylum seeker? Can you prove they are out to crucify you?

Modern-day nationalists have had to learn to be subtle (or

devious, if you prefer). Tommy Robinson* (b. 1982) is the co-founder of the English Defence League (EDL). In a 2014 interview he said: 'We need a new England where all religions and colours feel proud of our flag and recognize how important our identity and culture is.' Roughly translated, that is to say: 'We'll let them in if they promise to behave in a British manner.' Play cricket, eat haggis and learn to read road signs in Welsh, perhaps?

No, take a citizenship test. Not everyone can pass it. Even an ex-prime minister like David Cameron might struggle. He was asked by the American talk-show host David Letterman: '"Rule Britannia" is an iconic British song. Who wrote it?' Cameron replied, 'You're testing me there.' Yep, Lord Cameron, you are 100 per cent correct. He was testing you. So why did you have to go on and spoil your perfect record? Cameron hazarded, 'Edward Elgar?' Oops! If a prime minister can't pass a citizenship question, then what hope is there for Jesus or any other applicant to enter this sceptred isle?

A lot of the citizenship questions require a knowledge of British *history*, not British *life*. The suggestion is that if you learn Britannia's past, then you feel proud of our flag and recognize how important our identity and culture are. But why do people still sing, 'Britannia! rule the waves' when she clearly does not? Or, for that matter, A. C. Benson's lyrics (and Edward Elgar's music), written in 1902:

---

* His birth name is Stephen Yaxley-Lennon, but that doesn't sound so butch as Tommy Robinson, a leader of a 'street protest' movement, does it?

> Land of Hope and Glory, Mother of the Free,
> How shall we extol thee, who are born of thee?

Good citizens might point out that this anthem came from a land that had *killed* hope among certain indigenous peoples, won 'glory' at the barrels of its guns and suppressed the free around the world. The irony of the lyrics might be funny, if some people didn't still believe them and sing them heartily. They roar:

> Wider still and wider shall thy bounds be set;
> God, who made thee mighty, make thee mightier yet

Do they know what they are singing? There is a theory that A. C. Benson took those lines from the last will and testament of the racist empire-builder Cecil Rhodes. Rhodes bequeathed his (massive) wealth for the purpose of promoting 'the extension of British rule throughout the world'. He even appended a long list of territories which he thought should be colonized.

In 2006 a survey by the BBC revealed that 55 per cent of the English public would rather have 'Land Of Hope And Glory' than 'God Save The King/Queen' as their national anthem (English public, not British).

And maybe that is the nub of English nationalism: delusions of grandeur, given to it by the British Empire – an empire that was starting to disintegrate even when the lyrics were written as old Queen Vic died.

Britain and the Britons aren't the only country prone to narcissism. A 2018 survey asked students in thirty-five countries the nonsense question: 'What percentage contribution do you think your country made to world history?' If each country answered '2 or 3 per cent' then we'd get to a reasonable total. The combined total made up a 1,156 per cent contribution to world history. British students stood out, believing that Britain had contributed to 55 per cent of world history. Only Russian students, with 61 per cent, had a higher opinion of their own nation.

Every nation has a bias that comes through its teaching of history. We all think we're the greatest; no wonder there are wars. But what if Britons really are better than their rivals?

The French? They murder their monarchs. (Ignore Charles I, Edward II, Richard II, Anne Boleyn, Catherine Howard, Mary Queen of Scots et al.)

The Germans? Genocidal. (Ask a Tasmanian their view on that. Ah, sorry, you can't because the British wiped them out. Bet you weren't taught that in school.)

The Spanish? Ruthless conquistadors pillaging the world for slaves and gold. (Erm . . . British Empire? Worse still, Britain will invade you, but we don't want you over here.*)

And on it goes. Still. Britons are 'special', Britons are 'different', and Britain can manage perfectly well without having to live in harmony with the rest of the world. Even have the odd war . . . if they ask for it. As far back as John of Gaunt's 'sceptred isle' quote, we were dreaming of a long-dead past that never existed anyway.

---

* In *A Study in Scarlet*, Arthur Conan Doyle (1859–1930) has Dr Watson declare of London: 'that great cesspool into which all the loungers of the Empire are irresistibly drained'.

EPILOGUE

Maybe Britons need a less misty-eyed history, one that recognizes how much our own identity has in common with the people we spent so much time fighting. Maybe the world needs to step back to get a bit of perspective. As far back as the Moon? Someone who did that was US astronaut Frank Borman (1928–2023), who on returning to Earth in 1968 said, 'When you're finally up at the Moon looking back on Earth . . . you're going to get a concept that maybe this really is one world and why the hell can't we live together like decent people?'

Maybe we need to try and see ourselves as others see us. Otherwise, our leaders will continue to spout tosh like '*The British are special. The world knows it. In our innermost thoughts we know it. This is the greatest nation on Earth.*' Which British leader said that? Sir Anthony Charles Lynton Blair KG (Tony to his friends).

We have no enemies. People may speak unfamiliar languages, eat unfamiliar food or look a little different, but they share most of our genes. There are no foreigners, only people who live in another place. It's one of the things you learn when you read a bit of history. The same people who were enemies yesterday are often allies today, friends or family tomorrow. And the most important day in history is tomorrow. Always tomorrow.

FURTHER READING

CHAPTER 1

Mary Beard, *Emperor of Rome: Ruling the Ancient World*. Profile, 2023

Dan Jones, *In the Reign of King John: A Year in the Life of Plantagenet England*. Apollo, 2020

Peter Marshall, *Heretics and Believers: A History of the English Reformation*. Yale University Press, 2017

There are four surviving copies of the original 1215 Magna Carta, which you can visit at the British Library in London, at Salisbury Cathedral or at Lincoln Cathedral.

CHAPTER 2

Gildas, *The Ruin of Britain*, translated by Thomas Habington. IngramSpark, 2023

Cat Jarman, *The Bone Chests: Unlocking the Secrets of the Anglo-Saxons*. William Collins, 2023

The Anglo-Saxon Chronicle, translated by J. A. Giles. Independently published, 2021

CHAPTER 3

Geoffrey of Monmouth, *The History of the Kings of Britain*, translated by Lewis Thorpe. Penguin Classics, 1973

Neil Price, *The Children of Ash and Elm*. Allen Lane, 2020

Marc Morris, *The Norman Conquest*. Hutchinson, 2012

FURTHER READING

CHAPTER 4

Desmond Seward, *A Brief History of the Hundred Years War*. Robinson, 2003

Robert and Isabelle Tombs, *That Sweet Enemy: Britain and France, The History of a Love-Hate Relationship*. Pimlico, 2007

Adam Zamoyski, *Napoleon: The Man Behind the Myth*. William Collins, 2018

CHAPTER 5

Laurence Bergreen, *In Search of a Kingdom: Francis Drake, Elizabeth I, and the Perilous Birth of the British Empire*. Mariner Books, 2022

Robert Hutchison, *The Spanish Armada*. Weidenfeld & Nicolson, 2013

Colin Martin and Geoffrey Parker, *Armada: The Spanish Enterprise and England's Deliverance in 1588*. Yale University Press, 2022

CHAPTER 6

William Dalrymple, *The Anarchy: The Relentless Rise of the East India Company*. Bloomsbury Publishing, 2020

Thomas Pakenham, *The Boer War*. Abacus, 1991

Ben Wilson, *Empire of the Deep: The Rise and Fall of the British Navy*. Weidenfeld & Nicolson, 2013

CHAPTER 7

Rick Atkinson, *The British Are Coming: The War for America, Lexington to Princeton, 1775–1777*. Henry Holt, 2019

Kathleen Burk, *Old World, New World: The Story of Britain and America*. Little, Brown, 2009

David McCullough, *1776: America and Britain at War*. Penguin, 2006

CHAPTER 8

Orlando Figes, *Crimea: The Last Crusade*. Allen Lane, 2010

Simon Sebag Montefiore, *The Romanovs: The Story of Russia and its Empire 1613–1918*. Weidenfeld & Nicolson, 2016

Alfred Tennyson, *The Major Works*. Oxford University Press, 2009

CHAPTER 9

R. F. Foster, *Modern Ireland 1600–1972*. Penguin, 1988

Fearghal McGarry, *The Rising: Ireland, Easter 1916*. Oxford University Press, 2016

Patrick Radden Keefe, *Say Nothing: A True Story of Murder and Memory in Northern Ireland*. William Collins, 2018

CHAPTER 10

Juliet Gardiner, *The Blitz: The British Under Attack*. HarperPress, 2010

Katja Hoyer, *Blood and Iron: The Rise and Fall of the German Empire 1871–1918*. The History Press, 2021

Lyn Macdonald, *They Called it Passchendaele: The Story of the Battle of Ypres and of the Men Who Fought in it*. Michael Joseph, 1988

INDEX

Aboukir Bay, Battle of (1798) 110–11
Act of Union (1707) 201
Act of Union (1800) 201–2
Adamnan 64
Adams, Gerry 196
Adrian IV, Pope 186
Ælla, king of Northumbria, 71–2
Aengus, king of Munster 184
Æthelbert, king of Kent 58
Æthelfrith, king of Bernicia 59–60
Æthelred the Unready, king of the English 73, 74–5
Agincourt, Battle of (1415) 100–102
Alcuin (monk) 66, 67
Alençon, France 86–7
Alexander II, king of Scotland 81–2
Alexander II, Tsar 178
Alexander III, king of Scotland 82
Alexander VI, Pope 46–8
Alexander the Great 20

Alexandra Feodorovna, Tsarina 176, 177
Alexei, Tsar 170
Alfred the Great, King 72, 73
Allen, Captain William 162
Alphege, archbishop of Canterbury 70
Amalric, Arnaud 43
American Revolutionary War/War of Independence (1775–83) 103, 159–62
American Turtle (submarine) 161
Amherst, General Jeffrey 156–7
Anastasia, Grand Duchess 177, 178
Angles, the 53, 58, 199
Anglesey 28–9, 30
Anglo–Dutch Wars 140–45, 147–9, 151
Anglo-Saxon Chronicle 56–7, 66–7
Anglo-Saxons 53, 54, 56–8, 60, 91, 165
  monks 63–7
Anjou, Francis, Duke of 85

Anne, Queen 202–3
Arawak, the 121
Argos (sloop) 162
Arminius 23, 24–5, 26, 32
Arne, Thomas: 'Rule Britannia' 3, 226
Arthashastra (Kautilya) 17
Arthur, King 57
Arthur, Prince, duke of Brittany 41–2
Ashdown, Battle of (871) 73
Asser (monk) 72
Aston, Sir Arthur 190
Atrebates, the 25
Attacotti, the 35–6
Augustine of Canterbury, St 58–9, 60n
Augustus, Emperor 23–4

Balaclava, Battle of (1854) 174–5
Ball, Bishop Peter 65n
Baltimore, George Calvert, 1st Baron 156
Banda Islands, Indonesia 139, 140
Bangor (Wales), Monastery 59, 60
Baring-Gould, Sabine 12

INDEX

Barras, Paul-François, Vicomte de 107
Basing, Battle of (871) 73
Bath 8–9
Bayeux Tapestry 88
Beaker people, the 6, 8
Bede, Venerable 58, 64, 65–6, 67
Beecham, Sir Thomas 47
Benson, A. C.: 'Land Of Hope And Glory' 226–7
Benz, Bertha 200
Benz, Karl 200–201
Berry, Jean, Duke of 99
Bertric, king of Wessex 69
Betjeman, John: 'Slough' 216
Bismarck, Prince Otto von 113–14, 206, 207
Black Death 94–5, 96, 187
Black Hand, the (Serbian gang) 209
Bladud, Prince 8–9
Blair, Tony 120n, 229
Blake, William: 'And did those feet in ancient time . . .' 225
Blandina 38
Blas de Lezo, Don 133
Blitz, the/'Blitz Spirit' 216–17, 218, 219, 220, 222, 224
Boer Wars
    First (1880) 151
    Second (1899–1902) 151–2

Boleyn, Anne 49, 54
Borgia, Cesare 46, 47
Borgia, Lucrezia 46, 47
Borman, Frank 229
Borodino, Battle of (1812) 112–13
'Boston Massacre' (1770) 158–9
Boston Tea Party (1773) 159–60
Boudicca, Queen of the Iceni 29–32, 33
Bradford, William 157
Brendan, St 185
Brian Boru, King 80–81, 82
Brigantes, the 27
Brigid, St 185
Bristol: slaving ships 119
Britain/the British 1–12, 225–7, 228–9
    Angles 53, 58, 199
    Anglo-Saxons 53, 54, 56–8, 60, 63–4, 65, 91, 165
    burials 5–6, 9–12, 31–2
    Celts 2, 8–12, 15, 22, 25, 28, 59, 95, 184
    Christianity/the Church 39–45, 49–50, 58–9
    DNA 65
    English counties 57
    English language 53–4, 93–4
    Iron Age 8
    Magna Carta 44
    Normans 60, 86, 90–92, 94, 185–6, 201
    and the papacy 45–6, 48–50
    Romans 2–3, 8, 9, 10, 15, 16, 17–23, 25–31, 36–7, 54
    Saxons 53–5, 71, 73, 88, 90, 91
    slave trade 119, 122, 131, 138, 150, 156, 157, 203
    Stone Age 6
    Vikings 60, 63, 64, 65, 67–80, 90
    see also London; Scotland; Wales
Brithnoth (Saxon warrior) 70
British National Party (BNP) 4
Brodir (Viking leader) 80–81
Bruce, Edward 186, 187
Bunker Hill, Battle of (1775) 160
Burchard, Johann 46, 47, 48
burials
    Celtic 9–12
    Christian catacombs 38

Čabrinović, Nedeljko 209
Caesar, Julius 10, 16, 17–23, 27, 98
Calgacus, leader of the Picts 35

INDEX

Cameron, David 194n, 226
Camperdown, Battle of (1797) 149
Caratacus, king of the Catuvellauni 25, 26, 27
Cardigan, James Brudenell, 7th Earl of 174
Carlisle 92
Carlos, Prince of Asturias (Don Carlos) 124, 130
Carlyle, Thomas 108, 133
Carolina, Province of, America 156
Cartimandua, Queen of the Brigantes 27
Casabianca, Giocante 111
Casabianca, Captain Luc-Julien 111
Cassius Dio, Lucius (Dio Cassius) 30, 31
Cassivellauni, the 16–17, 19
Cassivellaunus, King 16, 19, 21, 22
Cathars, the 43–4
Catherine of Aragon 45, 49
Catherine, St 37
Catholic Church 37, 45, 50 *see also* papacy
Catuvellauni, the 25, 26
Cawdor, John Campbell, 1st Baron 109
Celestine, Pope 184
Celts 2, 8–12, 15, 22, 25, 28, 59, 95, 184

Celtic words 53–4
Chamberlain, Neville 216, 217
'Charge of the Light Brigade' 173–5
Charles I, of England 141, 170, 190
Charles II, of England 142, 143, 144, 145, 146, 156
Charles III ('the Simple'), of France 86
Charles IV, of France 95
Charles V, Holy Roman Emperor 49
Charles VI, of France 99–100
Charles VII, of France 99, 102, 103
Chatham Dockyards 143
Cherrill, Chief Superintendent 222
Chester 59–60
Christians/Christianity 36, 37–44, 58–60, 69
  see also Catholics; papacy, the; Protestants
Chubb, Cecil 7
Churchill, Winston 180, 214–15, 216, 217
Claiborne, Governor W. C. C. 163, 164
Clark, Kenneth 40
Claudius, Emperor 25, 26, 27
Clement VII, Pope 49

Clinton, Hillary 67–8
Clonmacnoise, Battle of (764) 185
Clontarf, Battle of (1014) 80–81, 82
Cnut, king of England 70–71, 75–7, 82
Cocles, Horatius 32
Coen, Jan Pieterszoon 139–40
Colchester 26, 30–31
Coldingham Monastery, Northumbria 64–5, 69
Coleridge, Samuel Taylor: 'France: An Ode' 105
Columba, St 184–5
Columbus, Christopher 119, 120–21
Concordat of London (1107) 40
Conn, Billy 17n
Constantine I, the Great 38
Cork, John Boyle, 5th Earl of 205
Coventry, bombing of (Second World War) 221
Crawford, Seaman Jack 149–50
Crécy, Battle of (1346) 95–6, 97
Cresswell, Nicholas 203
Crimean War (1853–6) 171–5
Cromwell, Oliver 141, 142, 183n, 190
Cruithne, the 34

INDEX

Culloden, Battle of (1746) 203
Cuthbert, St 91

Daily Express 224
Daimler car company 200
Dalriada, kingdom of 34
Danegeld 74–5
Danelaw 73
Dare, Virginia 155
David I, of Scotland 92
Denmark/Danes 3, 53, 54, 69, 70, 72–4, 75, 177n, 202, *see also* Vikings
Dickens, Charles: *A Tale of Two Cities* 104
Dinas, St 59
Disraeli, Benjamin 151, 152
Dogger Bank, Battle of (1781) 147
Dolgorukaya, Maria 169
Douglas, James 106
Dowth, Ireland: passage tomb 183–4
Doyle, Sir Arthur Conan: *A Study in Scarlet* 228n
Drake, Sir Francis 121, 122–4, 133
Druids 25, 28, 29
Dublin
   Easter Rising (1916) 193
   Nelson's Pillar 112
   and 'the Pale' 187–9
   slave market 93
   Wolf Tone's attack 190–91
   Vikings 80
Dubonni, the 26
Durham 90–91
Dutch, the 137ff.
   in America 157–8 *and n*
   conquest of Banda Islands 139, 140
   war with England 140–45, 147–9, 151, 152
   war with France 145–6
   war with Spain 137–8, 141, 142
Dutch East India Company 137–9, 140, 147, 151

Eagle, HMS 161
East India Company (British) 137, 138, 139, 140–41, 159
Ebba, Abbess of Coldingham Monastery 69
Edgar the Ætheling, Prince 90, 91
Edington, Battle of (878) 73
Edmund, king of East Anglia 68–9
Edmund Ironside 75–6
Edric Streona 76
Edric the Wild 90
Edward I, of England 34, 93
Edward III, of England 94, 95, 96, 97, 98
'Edward VI', of England 188
Edward the Confessor 77, 87
Effingham, Lord Charles Howard of 134
Eighty Years' War (1568–1648) 137
Elgar, Edward: 'Land Of Hope And Glory' 226–7
Elizabeth I 85–6, 119, 121–2, 124, 125, 126, 130, 133–4, 155, 170, 188, 189, 201
   and Drake 122–4
Elizabeth II 87
Ely, Isle of 91
Emmet, Robert 191
English Defence League (EDL) 226
Erhard, Ludwig 74
Esus (Celtic god) 10
European Community 115
Evelyn, John 146–7

Fandiño, Juan de León 132
Farage, Nigel 115
Fedelmid, king of Munster 185
Ferdinand, Archduke 209
Ferns (Ireland) Monastery 185
Ferrier, Christophe 106–7
Fields, W. C. 129
France/the French 5, 85ff., 200, 228
   and America 158, 164
   and Anglo–Dutch Wars 144–6, 147
   Cathars 43–4

INDEX

France/the French – *cont.*
and Entente Cordiale (1904) 208
Franco–Prussian War (1870–71) 114, 199
under de Gaulle 114–15
Hundred Years' War 94–9, 100–103
and Ireland 191
Joan of Arc 102–3
and King John 43, 45
last invasion of Britain 110 *and n*
Napoleonic Wars 162, *see also* Napoleon Bonaparte
and Nelson's victories 110–12
Normans 60, 78, 86–7, 90–94, 185–6, 201
Revolution 103–8, 179, 190
Romans 38
and Scotland 95, 98, 108
war with Russia (1854) 171–2
First World War 114, 176, 210, 211, 213
Second World War 114, 179, 180, 217
see also Gaul
Franco, General Francisco 215
Frederick (Fritz), Kaiser 206–7
Froissart, Jean 97
Funikov, Nikita 169

Fussell's Lodge, Wiltshire 6

Gage, General Thomas 160
Gaulle, Charles de 114, 115
Geoffrey of Monmouth 72
George I, of Britain 203
George III, of Britain 150, 161
George IV, of Britain: as Prince of Wales 150
George V, of Britain 176, 177 *and n*, 178
George, Prince of Denmark 202
Germanic tribes 23–5
Germany/Germans 53, 57, 114, 199ff., 228
and American War of Independence 161–2
and British royal family 201, 202, 203, 204, 205, 206
cars 200–201
Franco–Prussian War (1870–71) 114, 199
and Jews 207, 212, 215
Protestant Reformation 49
Thirty Years' War 131
under Wilhelm I and Wilhelm II 206–8
First World War 114, 175, 176–7, 200, 201, 205–6, 208, 209–10, 213, 214

Second World War 110, 114, 166, 179–80, 193, 201, 216, 217, 222–4, *see also* Hitler, Adolf
Gibraltar 133
Gilbert, Sir Humphrey 189
Gildas (monk) 36, 54, 55
Glorious Revolution (1688) 146–7
Godwinson, Tostig 78, 79
Goebbels, Joseph 214*n*
Gómez de Silva, Ruy, 1st Prince of Éboli 125
Grace, W. G. 212*n*
Grant, General Ulysses 165
Great Bengal Famine (1770) 159
Greece/Greeks 16, 39, 65, 124, 171
Gregory the Great, Pope 58
Guderian, General Heinz 216
Guillotin, Joseph-Ignace 105–6
guillotine, the 105–7
Guthrum (Danish chieftain) 73
Guy of Amiens: 'Song of the Battle of Hastings' 88–9
Gwynne, Nell 143

Haakon, king of Norway 82
Hadrian, Emperor 36
Hadrian's Wall 36, 54, 58

INDEX

Haiti: Arawak people 121
Halifax, Edward Wood, 1st Earl of 220
'Halifax Gibbet,' the 106
Hamilton, Evelyn 221
Hancock, Tony 44
Hardrada, Harold 77, 78–9
Harold (Godwinson), king of the English 77–80, 87, 88–9
Hastings, Battle of (1066) 87–90, 99
Hawkins, John 122
Hemans, Felicia Dorothea: 'Casabianca' 111–12
Hengist 54–5, 56–7
Henry I, of England 40
Henry II, of England 41, 92, 186
Henry III, of England 93
Henry IV, of England 93–4
Henry V, of England 99, 100, 102
Henry VII, of England 188
Henry VIII, of England 45, 46, 48, 49–50, 121, 169, 188
Hereward the Wake 91
hill forts 7, 9, 26
Hitler, Adolf 104*n*, 179, 212–13, 214–16, 217–18, 220
Horsa 54–5, 56
Howard, Catherine 169
Howard, Admiral Lord Charles 127

Hull, bombing of (Second World War) 221
Hundred Years' War (1337–60, 1415–53) 94, 95, 100, 103

Iceni, the 29–33
Industrial Revolution 172
Innocent III, Pope 40, 43–4
Innocent VIII, Pope 48
Ireland/the Irish 34, 53, 58, 183*ff*.
  Christianity 184–5, 196
  and Cromwell 142, 190
  Earl of Tyrone's rebellion (1593–1603) 130
  and the English 92, 94, 187–90, 192–6, 201
  famine and plague (fourteenth century) 186–7
  and the French 108
  Great Famine (1845) 191–2
  Home Rule 192–3
  Normans 185–6
  passage tombs 183–4
  Plantations 189
  Vikings 80–81, 82, 92, 185
  and First World War 206
  see also Dublin *and below*
Irish Republican Army (IRA) 193–5

Irish Republican Brotherhood (IRB) 193
Iron Age 8
Isabela, La (boat) 132
Isabella, of France 94
Ivan IV ('the Terrible'), Tsar 169–70
Ivar the Boneless 68

Jackson, General Andrew 163–4
Jacobites 147, 203
James I, of England 139, 140, 201
James II, of England 142, 146, 147
Jamestown, Virginia 156
Jellinek, Emil 200
Jellinek, Mercedes 200
Jenkins, Captain Robert 132, 133
Jerome, St 35–6
Jews, the 37, 207, 212, 214, 215
Joan of Arc 102–3
Joan, 'Lady of Wales' 93
John, king of England 40–45, 50 *and n*, 186
John II ('the Good'), of France 97
Johnson, Samuel 224
Jones, John Paul 148, 164
Julius II, Pope 48

Kautilya: *Arthashastra* 17
Keating, Geoffrey 183
Kentigern, St 185

INDEX

Kevin, St 185
Khrushchev, Nikita 180
King Philip's War (1675) 157
Kipling, Rudyard: 'Dane-Geld' 74
Knowth, Ireland: passage tomb 183–4

Lafitte, Jean 163–4
Langton, Stephen 40
Largs, Battle at (1262) 82
Laud (Peterborough) Chronicle 45
Laudabiliter (papal bull) 186
Lenin (Vladimir Ilyich Ulyanov) 104n, 178–9
Leo X, Pope 48–9
Leonardo da Vinci 49
Leopold, Prince of Hohenzollern 114
leprosy 8–9
Letterman, David 226
Lexington, Battle of (1775) 160
Lindisfarne Island 67, 69
'Lindow Man' 10–11
Liverpool: slaving ships 119
Llywelyn ap Gruffudd, 'Prince of Wales' 93
Llywelyn the Great 93
Loch Ness Monster, the 184–5
London 16, 21, 31–2
  Dorchester Hotel 220
  slaving ships 119
long barrows 6

Louis XIV, of France 144, 145
Louis XVI, of France 113
Louis XVIII, of France 113
Louis, Prince of France 45
Louis, Joe 17n
Lucan, George Bingham, 3rd Earl of 174, 192
Lud, King 16
Luther, Martin 49
Lyons: Christian persecution (AD 177) 38

MacErc, Fergus 34
MacMulrooney, Malachy, king of Ireland 185
MacMurrough, Dermot, king of Leinster 92
Madison, President James 164
Maelgwn 42–3
Magna Carta, the 44–5
Malcolm II, of Scotland 70–71
Malcolm III, of Scotland 91–2
Manchester City Football Club 223
Margaretta (schooner) 161
Maria, Grand Duchess 177, 178
Maria Manuela, Princess of Portugal 124
Marshall, George/ Marshall Plan 165–6
Martyr, Peter 121

Marvell, Andrew 144, 145
Mary I, of England 124, 125, 130, 170
Mary II, of England 146–7
Mary Stuart, Queen of Scots 125–6, 170
Maryland, USA 156
Matilda of Hay 42
Matthew of Paris 40–41
Maxentius, Emperor 37
Medina Sidonia, Alonso de Guzmán, 7th Duke of 127, 128
Mercedes-Benz cars 200–201
Michelangelo Buonarroti 49
Monkwearmouth Monastery 66
  abbot 64
Mons Graupius, Battle of (AD 84) 35
Morcar, Earl of Northumberland 78
Morgan, Captain Godfrey 175
Morrigan (Irish goddess) 9
Morrison, Herbert: bomb shelter 218
Mullins, William 156
Murphy, Peter 223
Mussolini, Benito 215

Napoleon Bonaparte 67, 104n, 105, 107–8, 110, 112–13, 139, 162, 171

INDEX

Native Americans 156–7, 158, 164–5
Neanderthals 5
Nelson, Lord Horatio 110–12, 150
Nero, Emperor 33, 37
Netherlands 137, *see* Dutch, the
New Hampshire Gazette 159
New Orleans, Battle of (1814) 163–4
New York 157
Newbold, Henry: 'Vitaï Lampada' 175, 210–11, 223
Newgrange, Ireland: passage tomb 183–4
Nicholas II, Tsar 175–8
Nicholas, Jemima 109–10
Nightingale, Florence 172–3
Nolan, Captain Louis 174–5
Normans 60, 86, 90–92, 94, 185–6, 201
Northey Island, Essex 70
Norway/Norwegians 63, 70, 76, 77, 79, 81, 82, *see also* Vikings

O'Connor, Rory 92
Oatley, Evelyn 221–2
Oldfield, DCS George 195
Olga, Grand Duchess 177, 178
Operation Barbarossa 179–80
Operation Sea Lion 217
Opium War, First (1839) 138
Ordovices, the 26
Orient, L' (ship) 111
Orkney Islands 82
Orsini, the 47
Ottoman Empire 171–2, 175
Owen, Wilfred 211
Oxford University: St John's College 75

Page, William 85
Paisley, Ian 196
Palladius 184
papacy, the/popes 36, 39, 40, 43–4, 45–9, 58, 184, 186
Parma, Alexander Farnese, Duke of 126, 128
Patrick, St 184, 185, 201
Paulinus (Roman general) 28–30, 31, 32–3
Peasants' Revolts 95
Pegwell Bay, Kent 18
Pelican, HMS 162
Pembroke, Richard, Earl of ('Strongbow') 92, 185–6
Pepys, Samuel 144
Pequots, the 157
Pétain, Marshal Philippe 114
Peter I, Tsar 170
Pett, Peter (Dockyard Commissioner) 143, 145
Philip II, of Macedon 20

Philip II, of Spain 124–6, 127, 129, 130
Philip VI, of France 94, 95, 96
Philip, king of the Wampanoags 157
Philip, Prince 124
Philip Augustus, of France 42
Pickle, HMS 112
Picts 33–5, 54, 55
Pliny the Younger 37
Plymouth Colony, Massachusetts 156
Poitiers, Battle of (1356) 96–7, 100, 101
popes *see* papacy
Prasutagus, King 29
Princip, Gavrilo 209, 213
Protestants 49, 50
Putin, Vladimir 180
Pytheas of Massalia 16

Ragnar Lodbrok 71–2
'Raid on the Medway' (1667) 143–5
Raphael (Raffaello Sanzio) 49
Rebecca (brig) 132
Reformation, Protestant 49
Rhodes, Cecil 151, 165, 227
Rhys ap Tewdwr 92–3
Richard I, of England 41
Richard II, of England 188

INDEX

Richard III, of England 40
Roanoke, North Carolina 155–6
Robert of Comines 90
Robespierre, Maximilien 105
Robinson, Tommy (Stephen Yaxley-Lennon) 226 *and n*
Rochester Castle, Kent 45
Rockefeller, John D. 165*n*
Roger of Wendover 69
Rollo (Viking) 86
Romans
    and Christianity 37–9
    in England 2–3, 8, 9, 10, 15, 16–23, 24, 25–6, 29–33, 36–7, 54, 58, 65
    in Scotland 33–6
    in Wales 26–9
Rome 22, 27, 36, 37, 38, 39, 40, 41, 48, 58, 115
Roosebeke, Battle of (1382) 99
Rosario (ship) 127
Rostand, Jean 140
Rowena 55
Royal Air Force (RAF) 217–18
Royal Charles, HMS 143, 144–5
Russell, W. H. 172
Russia 228
    Bolsheviks/Communists 176–7, 178–9
    and Britain 170–71, 172, 175
    Crimean War 172, 173–5
    and Napoleon 112–13
    Revolution (1917) 104*n*, 106
    First World War 175–7, 179, 209–10, 213, 214
    Second World War 179–80

St Albans 32
San Salvador (ship) 127
Saxons 53, 54–8, 71, 73, 88, 90, 91
Sayers, Dorothy L. 53
Scapula, Publius 26–7
Scota 34
Scotland/Scots
    and Act of Union (1707) 201
    Celtic language 53
    Christianity 184
    under Cnut 71
    flag 201
    and France 95, 98, 108
    in Ireland 186–7, 189, 192
    Jacobite rebellions 147, 203
    'The Maiden' (mechanical axe) 106
    and Mary Queen of Scots 125–6, 142, 170
    and Norman Conquest 91–2, 94
    and Norwegians 81–2
    Picts 33–5, 36, 54, 55
    Romans 33–6
    Scots 1, 34, 54, 55
    and Stuarts 142, 201, 203
    and Vikings 81
    and First World War 206
Serbia 209–10
Seven Years' War (1756–63) 171
Shakespeare, William
    Henry V 100, 101
    King John 3
    Richard II 2, 43, 228
Shaw, George Bernard 207
Shelley, Percy Bysshe 67, 91*n*
Shetland Islands 82
Sidney, Sir Henry 188–9
Sidney, Sir Philip 188
Silures, the 26–7
slave trade/slaves
    in America 156, 157, 161, 164, 203
    British 119, 122, 131, 138, 150, 156, 157
    and the Church 69
    Dutch 139, 140
    Irish 93
    Roman 10, 19, 58
    Spanish 119–21, 122
    Viking 68, 69
    Welsh 92–3
Society of United Irishmen 190–91
Song of Roland 88

INDEX

South Carolina, USA 157
Spain/the Spanish 114, 119*ff.*, 137, 228
   Armada 119, 126–30, 133–4
   Inquisition 119, 125, 137
   in North America 157, 158, 164
   and slavery 119–21, 122
   treasure ships 122–4
   war with Britain 98, 126–33, 158, 164
   war with the Dutch 137–8, 141, 142
   see also Philip II
Spectator 68*n*
'Splendid Isolation' 171
Spragge, Admiral Edward 146
Stalin, Joseph 179
Stamford Bridge, Battle of (1066) 79–80, 82
Stamp Act (1765) 158
Statute of Rhuddlan (1284) 93
Stendhal 67
Stephen, king of England 43
Stone Age 6–7, 183
Stone of Destiny 34–5
Stonehenge 6–7
Strachey, Lytton 173
Strand, The 214–15
Stubbs, John 85
Sudetenland, the 215–16
Sun Tzu: *The Art of War* 72–3
Sunderland: Mowbray Park 150*n*

Sussex, Thomas Radclyffe, 3rd Earl of 188
Sweden 63, 177*n*

Tacitus 15, 22, 27, 28, 29, 30, 31, 35*n*
Taghmon (Ireland) Monastery 185
Taillefer (minstrel) 88
Tandey, Henry 211–13
Tate, Colonel William 110*n*
Tatiana, Grand Duchess 177, 178
Telupa, Prince Boris 169
Tennyson, Alfred, Lord: 'The Charge of the Light Brigade' 174, 175
Teutates (Celtic god) 10
Teutoburg Forest, Battle of the (AD 9) 23, 24, 32
Texel, Battle of (1673) 146
Thanet, Kent 55
Thatcher, Margaret 29, 32
Thirty Years' War (1618–48) 130–31
Thomson, James: 'Rule Britannia' 3
Times, The 172
Tone, Wolfe 190–91
Tordhelbach 81
Toronto, American capture of (1813) 162–3
Trafalgar, Battle of (1805) 112
Trajan, Emperor 37

Trautmann, Bert 222–4
Treaty of Paris (1783) 162
Tyrone, Hugh O'Neill, Earl of 130

Uhtred, Earl of Northumbria 71
Ulyanov, Alexander 178
Union Jack (flag) 201
United States of America 155*ff.*
   British settlers 155–8
   the Dutch 147, 157–8 *and n*
   1812–1814 wars 162–3
   the Irish 192
   Native Americans 156–7, 158, 164–5
   Navy 148
   slaves 156, 157, 161, 164, 203
   Revolutionary War/War of Independence (1775–83) 103, 147, 148, 158–62
   and Russia 180
   First World War 165
   Second World War 165–6
Urach, Dietrich 45–6

Varus, Publius Quinctilius 23–4
Vasilchikova, Anna 169
Victoria, Princess 207
Victoria, Queen 176, 205, 207, 227
Victory, HMS 112

Vikings
  in England 60, 63, 64, 65, 67–80, 90
  in France 86
  in Ireland 80–81, 82, 92, 185
  in Scotland 81–2
  in Wales 92–3
Virginia, USA 156
Vortigern, king of the Britons 54, 55–6, 57
Vortimer 55

Wales/the Welsh
  and Act of Union (1707) 201
  Christians 59, 60
  and England 41, 42, 58, 92–3, 94, 95, 201, 206
  language 53, 60
  and Napoleon 108–10, 139
  Romans 26–9
  soldiers at Agincourt 101–2
  Tudors 92–3, 201
  Vikings 92–3
Walpole, Sir Robert 131
Wampanoag, the 157
Wappinger, the 158
War of the Austrian Succession (1740–48) 171
War of Jenkins' Ear 132–3
Ward, Judith 195
Wars of the Three Kingdoms 142
Washington, DC: British attack (1814) 163
Washington, George 160, 161–2
Waterford, Ireland 92
Waterloo, Battle of (1815) 113
Watling Street, Battle of (AD 61) 32–3
Wellington, Arthur Wellesley, Duke of 113
Wellum, Geoffrey 222
Wessex 57, 73–4
Western Flying Post 204
Weymouth, Dorset 71
White, John 155
Wighill (servant) 71
Wilberforce, William 150
Wilhelm I, Kaiser 199, 206
Wilhelm II, Kaiser 205–6, 207–8, 209–10, 214
William I ('the Conqueror') 78, 80, 86–90, 91, 92, 94, 98, 99
William III, of Orange 146–7
William of Malmesbury 55
  Gesta Regum Anglorum 89
William of Poitiers 86
Wilson, Bob 224
Wordsworth, William 105, 106
  The Prelude 104
First World War 114, 131, 165, 175, 176–7, 179, 192–3, 200, 201, 205–6, 208–14
Second World War 114, 165–6, 179–80, 201, 213, 215–24

Yeltsin, Boris 178
York 65, 77–8, 79, 90

ABOUT THE AUTHOR

Terry Deary is the author of 340 published books including the acclaimed Horrible Histories series, selling over 38 million books in 45 languages. The series has been adapted for theatre, museum exhibitions and a major CBBC television series, which has gone on to win several Children's BAFTA awards and a British Comedy Award for best sketch show – the first children's show ever to win.

Terry was conferred with an honorary Doctorate of Education by Sunderland University in 2000. He currently lives in County Durham with his wife, Jenny, and is an avid road runner in his spare time.

REVOLTING
A short history of riots, rebellions and revolutions

From the *Sunday Times* bestselling author Terry Deary

It is a truth universally acknowledged that the rich and powerful always look after their own and the working people are always revolting. But every now and again, a new group actually manages to seize power, and it changes history.

Horrible Histories author Terry Deary takes readers on a hilarious, gruesome and eye-opening journey through some of the most significant revolts and uprisings that have happened around the world, revealing what we have learned along the way (and what we are doomed to repeat).

From the peasants to the slaves, the suffragists to the civil rights activists, *Revolting* celebrates the resilience and determination of those who dared to challenge the status quo.